RACE, RACISM, AND, SLAVERY

(The Biblical Perspective)

D1570419

By Tom Logan

DEDICATION

This book is dedicated to my lovely wife Jan who has inspired, encouraged, and supported me in this pursuit; and who has changed my life for the better from the day we first met; and our two beloved daughters Victoria and Elizabeth.

Acknowledgments

I give my sincere thanks to my lovely wife Jan who has supported me through this endeavor and without whose love and sacrifice, this book would not be possible. I also thank Brandon and Elizabeth Joyner, who kept me supplied by immediately ordering various reference materials needed for research; and Victoria Logan, who provided me with services and necessities which allowed me to devote full attention to completing this writing.

Also, I would like to thank my sister, Mary Ellen Joyner who prompted me to undertake this project by asking a simple question, "Tom, when are you going to write a book?"

Finally, I would like to thank Eminey Gullmaz, Zack Harris, and all the great people at Book Marketeers for having the courage to take on a sensitive subject on which the current culture has such divergent views. We pray this nation, and the world will be much better as a result of this work.

SOME QUESTIONS THIS BOOK ANSWERS

What does the Bible say about race and racism?

Does the Bible support slavery?

Why are some people black and others white?

Is the United States Systemically Racist?

What is Critical Race Theory and Wokeness?

Should descendants of slaves be paid repatriation?

How has Race, Racism, and Slavery affected the church?

What is Black Liberation Theology?

Is Christianity the "white man's religion?"

What is the solution for Racism and Wokeness in the church?

INTRODUCTION

I grew up in Summerville, South Carolina during the 1950s and 60s. Summerville was a small but rapidly expanding town that was completely segregated right up into the late 60s. My elementary and high school years were spent in a segregated school up to the time I graduated in 1968. I was the youngest of 12 children, 8 girls and 4 boys. Being the youngest, some of my older sisters were more like mother figures to me than sisters.

We grew up in a Christian home and our parents required us to go to Sunday school every Sunday and participate in various church activities. In Sunday school, I learned the basic Bible stories (Creation, Adam & Eve, Noah and the Ark, the Christmas story, Crucifixion, etc.) but didn't really make the connection as to what this was all about, at least from an eternal perspective. I knew that I had to obey my parents, respect all adults, don't lie or steal, along with all the other moral principles instilled in most kids at that time. I was taught and frequently reminded that I was to be good if I wanted to go to heaven when I died. My parents also placed a very strong emphasis on getting a good education.

Being black and living in a black community, I had very little interaction with white people while growing up but I understood what racism was. This was easy to comprehend because racism and segregation-type topics were talked about in the news, on radio and TV, and in general conversations among adults. It was generally known and widely understood that blacks and whites were different, and were not to mix with each other, at least not in any intimate fashion.

Among many whites, it appeared that the general consensus was that blacks were inferior and lazy, and the general consensus among blacks was that whites were racist and evil. This was deemed true for some time even after the Civil Rights Bill was passed into law in 1964. Furthermore, there were many assaults by some whites against blacks, and several racist activities that took place during the fifties and sixties (Referred to by some as the Civil Rights Era) that attracted national and international attention. Four of these highly publicized, racist activities were severe, tragic, and left an indelible impact on my young mind and a bad feeling about people in the white race in general. These four events were as follows:

On September 15, 1963, at the 16th Street Baptist Church in Birmingham, Alabama. Ku Klux Klan members set off a bomb, that killed four little black girls and injured more than 20 other church members. There were many church bombings and burnings during this period, and this was the third church bombing in Birmingham in eleven days as churches were the meeting place for Civil Rights Leaders and others seeking civil rights for African Americans.

On June 21, 1964, three Civil Rights Workers were tortured and murdered by Ku Klux Klan members in Mississippi. The three young men had traveled to Neshoba County from the Freedom Summer orientation in Oxford, Ohio to investigate the burning of Mt. Zion Methodist Church. Their bodies were found more than a month later buried in an earthen dam. While dragging the river searching for the boys, authorities uncovered the bodies of eight other African Americans. This event was the true background story for the award-winning movie, "*Mississippi Burning.*" I vividly remember this event and our parents being afraid for us, continuously telling us to be careful where we go and what we do.

On February 8, 1968, three students from South Carolina State College (SCSC, now University) were shot and killed by police on the Campus in Orangeburg, South Carolina. Twenty-eight others were wounded but none of the students were armed. Tensions had been escalating between students and police as students attempted to desegregate the All-Star Bowling establishment in downtown Orangeburg. At the time, I had already enrolled in SCSC and was making plans to live on campus during the fall of that year.

On April 4,1968 Civil Rights Leader, Dr. Martin Luther King Jr. was assassinated as he stood on the balcony of the Loraine Motel in Memphis, Tennessee. Dr. King had gone to Memphis to support the rights of African American sanitation workers who had staged a walkout to protest unequal wages and working conditions. This event shocked the nation and brought national and international attention to racial problems in the South and other parts of the country.

There were many other such violent acts, mostly on a smaller scale, that were carried out against blacks during this time. However, these four stuck with me and further confirmed the mindset I had about whites all along. In my mind, these people were evil, not just some of them, *all* of them. After graduating from high school in 1968, I attended SCSC in Orangeburg, South Carolina. SCSC was one of the historically black colleges and universities (HBCU) and there were very few whites there, none of whom I got to know or had any contact with, other than a few white teachers. When I graduated from South Carolina State College in 1972, like many southern blacks, I headed north where I lived in New York for the next twelve years. During this time, I worked as a bookkeeper and tax preparer while I attended graduate school at Long Island University (LIU).

LIU was a predominantly white university, with a fairly large number of foreign students from Europe, India, China, and Africa. Here. I began to interact with many people of different races and ethnic backgrounds and formed relationships with various whites. In January 1981, I began a career as a Revenue Agent with the Internal Revenue Service (IRS) and it was here where I really began acting and interacting with whites on a personal and professional level.

Many of these people became close friends of mine as we worked together, lunched together, and had wonderful, enjoyable times together. It wasn't long before I realized that whites were not the evil and racist people that I was led to believe while growing up. I realized that my perception of white people was misguided and grossly inaccurate. I learned that white people were just like everyone else and wanted the same out of life as everyone else, family, education, careers, peace, safety, security, happiness, etc.

Even though I grew up in a Christian home, I stopped going to church in my early teens but in 1984 I was drawn back into the church. The church into which I was drawn was a relatively large international church with congregations all over the world and members of virtually every background and ethnic group. I became far more involved with my white brothers and sisters in Christ at this time and developed a bond with many. As I began studying the Bible and growing spiritually, I learned that Jesus taught His followers to love everyone, even our enemies (Matt. 5:44-45).

Over the years, as I observed other Christians throughout the United States, I detected elements of anger and ill-will among some blacks and whites. This was usually in the form of conversations and not always overt or ostentatious but was quite easy for me to recognize because I harbored these same sentiments at one time too. Although by this time, I had a different godly perspective of others, whites, blacks, and everyone else. I had always thought that the primary problem was whites being prejudiced against blacks, but I later observed that it was also blacks prejudiced against whites. In fact, in many situations, I see more cases of hatred of blacks against whites than the other way around.

I have come to the realization that even today, in the black church, many black Christians have a lingering, prejudicial view of whites even to the extent where it has impeded the love, unity, and closeness that Jesus told us to have with each other. Again, this is mostly played out in words and body language rather than actual physical action, but it is noticeable to anyone who has experienced this mindset before.

In the secular world, the concept of racism has evolved into many other facets with new terms and philosophies like, social justice, critical race theory, wokeness, white privilege, white supremacy, and has now become a part of the makeup of the church. Even from the pulpit, I've observed some black preachers, whether consciously or subconsciously, delivering messages with underlying racial overtones. Then there are those Christian preachers and teachers, even though less common, who speak blatantly outright that whites are racists, and they need to repent of their sins against blacks.

I learned that while some whites are racist, the vast majority are not and at the same time, there are many blacks that are racist which many Christians fail to talk about in this politically correct society. I learned that this is a situation that the enemy of Christianity and the world is behind (Rev. 12:9; Ephes. 6:12). I concluded that racism is not a white against black problem as I thought earlier in life and as many thinks today, it is not a black against white problem, it is a spiritual problem. A spiritual problem that can only be resolved with a spiritual solution.

This book is being written in the hopes that it will help all my brothers and sisters in the body of Christ get a deeper and better understanding of the truth of the racial disparities and problems, the source behind it all, and the critical importance of why we should view this entire situation from a biblical perspective. We are also publishing this book in the hopes that those who are not of the Christian faith will come to an understanding that the only way there will be peace on racial and other such issues is through the Prince of Peace, Jesus Christ.

Chapter 1 sets forth some of the traditional arguments for the reliability of the Bible. Since all of our understanding comes from God (Job 32:8) and we are to live by every word that comes from God (Matt. 4:4), we believe that we should begin by showing that we can trust the Bible and if we put forth an effort to live by the Bible, the racial problems will at the very least be substantially diminished.

Chapter 2 explains how God our Creator is One but diverse in nature (Father, Son, and Holy Spirit), loves diversity and showed diversity throughout His creation. These diversifications in mankind are sufficient to remind us that we as human beings are not responsible for what God has made us in terms of race and skin color.

In Chapter 3 we define race, explain how we are different and why we have different skin colors. We also show that internally, we are not as different as one may think, the real difference in all human beings is less than one percent, and that race is a concept developed by man, not God.

Chapter 4 provides the biblical perspective on race and highlights examples of racism in the Old and New Testaments.

Chapter 5 explains the definition of systemic racism and explains why the United States does not technically fit this definition. This Chapter also includes a basic analysis of the Declaration of Independence and the U.S. Constitution to show that these documents are based on the Bible and the United States was started as a Christian nation.

In Chapter 6 we bring out various facts centered around *Race, Racism, and Slavery* to enable the reader to be more aware of plain truths that should be used when assessing various racial issues.

Chapter 7 brings out situations and various consequences that occur when we are not being truthful and honest, and seeing these issues from a biblical perspective.

We conclude with Chapter 8 by demonstrating how this concept of racism, liberalism, and wokeness has had a negative impact on Christians and the Church, and gives some helpful advice to pastors, teachers, black and white Christians, and those who are not of the Christians faith, on how we can improve these problems. All Scriptures used in this book are from the New King James Version unless otherwise designated. Since racism, liberalism, and wokeness are all based on Marxism, these words are sometimes used interchangeably and not always simultaneously.

TABLE OF CONTENTS

CHAPTER 1
THE BIBLE - THE ANSWER TO IT ALL

All Scripture is given by inspiration of God, and is profitable for doctrine, for reproof, for correction, for instruction in righteousness (2 Timothy 3:16).

The Reliability of the Bible

Because we are taking a biblical perspective on *Race, Racism, and Slavery,* we believe it is most helpful to begin with demonstrating that the Bible has more than ample evidence to show that it is from God and therefore reliable. Many readers of the Bible believe that it is just another book, that it is for people in ancient history and/or it is full of errors. However, neither of these are true. There are at least five classic arguments that we can make to show the authenticity and reliability of the Bible. They are manuscripts, archaeology, fulfilled prophecy, science, and the testimony of Jesus. Below we will provide examples of some of the arguments from each.

Manuscripts

Manuscripts are copies of the original writings since, with all ancient writings, originals have not withstood the ravages of time. Therefore, when historians and other scholars research a document to confirm its authenticity and validity, they use manuscripts to help in this pursuit. The more manuscripts there are and the earlier the manuscripts are to the time of the event, the more reliable the document.

You can understand by thinking of an event that had a significant impact on the United States. For example, the attack on the World Trade Center in New York, the Pentagon in Washington, DC, and the crash of the airliner in Shanksville, PA, all occurred on September 11, 2001.

If you were conducting research and questioned someone as to the details of that event on, say, 2005, they are likely to provide you with much more accurate information than someone whom you questioned in 2016 which would be 15 years from the date of the original event. In other words, the closer your research to the date of the event, the more valid your findings will be. Likewise, the closer manuscripts are to the date of an event, the more accurate those documents would be. Furthermore, the more people you questioned in 2005, the easier it will be to validate their testimony. This is because you would have more sources by which you can check and cross-check for accuracy.

The same principle applies when scholars research the authenticity of the Bible. The questions are (1) how close was the testimony to the actual events; and (2) how many manuscripts were there. In researching for the authenticity of the Bible, historians found more than 5,700 Greek manuscripts of the New Testament[1]. This is incredible when you consider that most other books from the ancient world were considered valid based on about 10 or 20 manuscripts. Furthermore, the New Testament manuscripts were

---

[1] Norman L. Geisler, *A Popular Survey of the New Testament*, 19

found to be much earlier (Closer to the time of the event) than other books from antiquity.

Most other books have been considered authentic and used in public schools, colleges, universities, and other educational institutions with manuscripts created one thousand years after the book was composed (see Figure 1.1).[2]

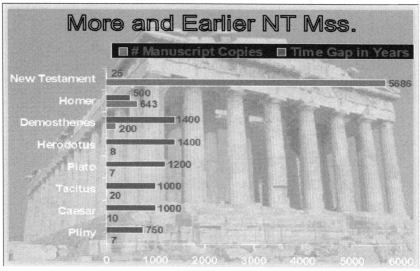

Figure 1.1. Reliability of the New Testament Documents

What these findings mean is that if the Bible is deemed unreliable, all of the writings shown in this chart, as well as other writers in antiquity must be discredited for being invalid. We are focusing on the New Testament here because if the New Testament is found to be authentic, the Old Testament is also reliable since the New Testament confirms the authenticity of the Old Testament. Even so, the Old Testament also has impressive amounts of

---

[2] Ibid. 20

manuscripts, listing more than 700, including those found in the Dead Sea Scrolls.[3]

There are also substantial amounts of non-Christian sources found outside of the New Testament. There are several sources but two of the best sources for this information are F.F. Bruce, *Jesus and Christian Origins Outside the New Testament* and Gary Habermas' *The Historical Jesus*. Several non-Christian writers at the time include authors such as the Jewish historian Josephus, Tacitus, Suetonius, Thallus, the Jewish Talmud and others. These sources confirm the following biblical information about Jesus.[4]

- Jesus was from Nazareth.
- He lived a virtuous life.
- He performed unusual feats.
- He introduced new teaching contrary to Judaism.
- He was crucified under Pontius Pilate.
- His disciples believed he rose from the dead.
- His disciples denied polytheism.
- His disciples worshipped him.
- His teachings spread rapidly, and the number of his disciples quickly grew.
- His followers believed they were immortal.
- His followers had contempt for death.
- His followers renounced material goods

The fact that these corroborations came from outside sources speaks volumes to the authenticity of the New Testament.

Archaeology

---

[3] Josh McDowell, *The New Evidence that Demands A Verdict*, 72.
[4] Norman L. Geisler, *A Popular Survey of the New Testament*, 34.

Archaeologists have also found an abundance of convincing evidence for the authenticity of the Bible, thus the reliability of Scripture. Many archaeological discoveries have confirmed people, places, events, and writings found in the Scriptures. Moreover, there has never been an archaeological find that refuted or disproved any biblical claim or doctrine. Instead, there has been abundant archaeological evidence that supports the historical reliability of the New and Old Testaments. There has never been an Archaeological discovery that refutes the Bible while there are thousands of discoveries that have supported the Bible.[5]

An example of archaeological evidence relating directly to Jesus:[6]

- Jesus' Home Town--Excavation at Nazareth
- Pilate Inscription--Pontius Pilate's name in stone (1st cent.).
- Caiaphas Inscription--High Priest of Jesus' time (1st cent.).
- Yohanan--a Crucifixion Victim from c. A.D. 70 (found 1968).
- The Nazareth Decree--slab of stone with decree from Emperor Claudius (A.D. 41-54) not to move bodies under pain of death.
- Numerous other cites—These relate to his birth, life, travels, teachings and acts.

An Example of biblical structures that have been found.[7]

- Ruins from the ancient cities of Sodom and Gomorrah.
- Discovery of Ebla, once a prestigious city that ruled the Far East, with more than 15,000 tables and fragments confirming biblical names, geographical locations, biblical events, and names of patriarchs found in the Bible.

---

[5] Nelson Glueck, *Rivers in the Desert,* 31.
[6] Norman L. Geisler, *A Popular Survey of the New Testament*, 35.
[7] Josh McDowell, *The New Evidence that Demands A Verdict,* 94-95.

- Ruins verifying the destruction of the city of Jericho and the manner in which the wall fell.

Regarding Jericho, between 1930 and 1936, British Archaeologist John Garstang and his team uncovered such amazing finds that it led writer Bryant Wood to write the following analysis in the *Biblical Archaeology Review* regarding the ruins of the city.

1. The city was strongly fortified (Josh. 2:5, 7, 15; 6:5, 20).
2. The attack occurred just after harvest time in the spring (Josh. 2:1; 3:15; 5:16).
3. The inhabitants had no opportunity to flee with their foodsheds (Josh. 6:1).
4. The siege was short (Josh. 6:15).
5. The walls were leveled, possibly by an earthquake (Josh. 6:20).
6. The city was not plundered (Josh. 6:17, 18).
7. The city was burned (Josh. 6:24).

These are just some of the archaeological discovers but there are thousands more as attested to by Scholar and Archaeologist Donald J. Wiseman:

"The geography of Bible lands and visible remains of antiquity were gradually recorded until today more than 25,000 sites within this region and dating to Old Testament times, in their broadest sense, have been located ...[8]

There are also the now famous Dead Sea Scrolls which were discovered in eleven caves along the northwest shore of the Dead Sea beginning in 1949. These scrolls were found in clay pots located in caves and confirmed the reliability of the Old Testament. They contained manuscripts dating from as early as the third century B,

---

[8] Donald J. Wiseman, *"Archaeological Confirmation of the Old Testament,"* in C.F.H. Henry, *Revelation and the Bible, Contemporary Evangelical Thought,* 1.

C. to the first Century A.D.; containing some 700 manuscripts including the entire book of Isaiah and fragments of every book of the Old Testament with the exception of Esther. [9] All of these finds confirmed the information we have in our Bibles today.

Fulfilled Prophecy

There is nothing like Bible prophecy that has been fulfilled to verify the authenticity and reliability of the Bible. This is because, even though there are skeptics who have tried to dispute the evidence for fulfilled prophecy, all of their attempts and efforts have been debunked. There is approximately 27% of the entire Bible devoted to prophecy including 28.6% in the Old Testament and 21.6% in the New Testament.[10] To determine the authenticity of Scripture, that is the Bible has a divine origin, we can review specific prophecies in the Bible, then research valid historical records outside of the Bible to see if these prophecies actually occurred. Bible prophecy must meet at least three criteria to support its supernatural origin and divine nature:

1. It must be more than just a vague guest, conjecture or reading of trends.
2. It must deal with human contingencies that are normally unpredictable (e.g., scientific predictions dealing with projections based on regularities in nature like the prediction of an eclipse do not count).
3. It is a highly unusual event not normally expected (This is sometimes demonstrated in the length of time between the

---

[9] Norman L. Geisler, *Baker Encyclopedia of Christian Apologetics.* 187.
[10] H. Wayne House & Randall Price, *Charts of Bible Prophecy*, 17.

prediction and the event occurring and sometimes the uniqueness of the event itself).[11]

There are two broad categories of Bible prophecy, messianic (prophecies concerning Jesus) and non-messianic (all other prophecies).

Jesus reminds us that, "Now I tell you before it comes, that when it does come to pass, you may believe that I am *He* (John 13:19)." Jesus alone has fulfilled more than 300 prophecies. For example, Isaiah wrote approximately 700 BC and prophesied that Jesus would be born of a virgin and would give hearing to the deaf and sight to the blind (Isaiah 7:14; 29:18); Micah who also wrote approximately 700 BC said Jesus would be born from the Tribe of Judah and in Bethlehem (Micah 5:2-5); Moses wrote that Jesus would be born of the seed of Abraham 1,500 years before Jesus was born (Genesis 12:3, 7). These prophecies were made hundreds of years before Jesus was born yet, all of these prophecies were fulfilled in the birth of Jesus around 4 to 6 BC as confirmed in the New Testament, and we've seen evidence that the New Testament is reliable. Furthermore, there are also non-biblical historical sources (Ignatius, bishop of Antioch, Encyclopedia Britannica, Flavius Josephus, etc.) to verify the fulfillment of these prophecies.[12]

The Bible shows an amazing prophecy made by Daniel, most of which already occurred and verified in history. The rest of the prophecy is to occur in the future but preparations are currently being made in Europe for the fulfillment of the remaining parts of those prophecies.

---

[11] Norman L. Geisler, *Baker Encyclopedia of Christian Apologetics.* 609-610.
[12] Ibid. 609-613.

The book of Daniel mentions four world-ruling empires (Daniel 2 and 7). These world-ruling empires were (1) Babylonian Empire (2) Persian Empire (3) Greco-Macedonian Empire, and (4) Roman Empire, in that order. Each succeeding empire defeated and replaced the prior empire, except for the last which was the Roman Empire. The Roman Empire was not defeated by a succeeding empire but lost its status as an Empire by destroying itself from within with political division, sinful, riotous living, and a series of other complex events.

According to Daniel Chapters 2 and 7, just before the Second Coming of Jesus Christ, this Roman Empire would be revived in the form of ten nations (Ten Kingdoms) or ten groups of nations, but Jesus will destroy it at His Second Coming (Dan. 2:31-35). History shows that all of this happened precisely as prophesied with the revived Roman Empire yet future. Interestingly enough however, a careful review of history and current world events show that many efforts have been taken to revive the Roman Empire over the past century.

Today, practically all prophecy scholars agree that the European Union (EU) is the economic and geopolitical foundation of what will ultimately materialize into the revived Roman Empire. There are several factors that support this belief, including but not limited to:

- The EU is currently the world's largest market.
- The EU has 27 countries (2021) and almost 450 million citizens (Beginning of 2019).
- The EU has its own currency.
- The EU has its own flag and national anthem
- The EU has a common foreign and security policy currently working at achieving greater political unity in this area.

- The EU has its own central bank, the ECB.
- The EU has its own Border Control and Coast Guard
- The EU has the beginnings of its own
- The EU Spy Agency (EU INTCEN)

Whatever one may believe, it is certain that the European Union is in a better position to fulfill the role of a revised Roman Empire than any other group of nations on the European continent today. We can be certain this prophecy will be fulfilled.

One favorite fulfilled prophecy for many prophecy scholars and students is when God promised the Jewish people that He would scatter them from their land all over the earth (Deut. 4:25-27, Psalms 106:24-27). This massive dispersion of the Jews took place in 70AD when General Titus of Rome came into Jerusalem, sacked the city, destroyed the temple, and the Jews were scattered to the four corners of the earth, just as God had prophesied (Zach. 2:6).

While the prophesies were made hundreds of years earlier (In the case of Moses, 1500 years earlier), history shows this event took place just as predicted. But God also told the Jews that He would gather them from the four corners of the earth and bring them back into their homeland in the end time (Eze. 20:34, Isa. 11:11-12). The prophecy that God will regather the Jewish people in the end time and bring them back into their homeland is mentioned more than any other prophecy in the Old Testament. [13]

In 1897 a Jewish political activist by the name of Theodor Herzl established the Zionist movement and the Jews slowly began coming back into Israel. After World War II and the holocaust, there was a large influx of Jews into Israel. Jews came into Israel from Russia, Germany, and other areas of Eastern Europe.

---

[13] David Reagan, *Living on Borrowed Time,* 130.

Thousands of Jews also came from Ethiopia and other areas, today totaling 180 different countries.[14] Finally, on May 14, 1948, David Ben-Gurion, first Prime Minister of Israel announced to the world the creation of the state of Israel (see Figure 1.2). This is one of the most amazing prophecies in the Bible! After 2,000 years, a race or ethnic group of people after having been scattered all over the world, were brought right back into the land that God promised them, with the same customs, and many speaking the same Hebrew language that God gave their ancestors, Abraham, Isaac, and Jacob. This fulfilled prophecy made a believer of many skeptics and critics, and it also verified the authenticity of the Bible. [15]

Figure 1.2 David Ben-Gurion Reading Israel's Declaration of Indepeence in Independence Hall (May 14, 1948).

---

[14] David Reagan, *Israel in Bible Prophecy, Past, Present & Future*, 87-94.
[15] Ibid. 95.

There are many more prophecies, messianic and non-messianic that were fulfilled precisely as prophesied, right to the letter. An honest reader of these prophesies and their fulfillment would have to admit that the Bible has divine origins and as such, is 100% reliable.

Science

Many people believe that there is a conflict between science and the Bible or that science disproves the Bible. This is deeply flawed thinking as science actually confirms the authenticity of the Bible in a number of ways. Consider the examples below.

In the first book, first Chapter and first verse of the Bible, we read: In the beginning God created the heavens and the earth (Gen. 1:1). For thousands of years, man believed that the earth always existed (some still do). However, modern science tells us today that the universe had a beginning. There are more than five different lines of evidence that the universe had a beginning and scientists refer to this beginning by calling it the Big Bang. In other words, scientist have evidence that the universe actually came into existence from nothing. This is precisely what the Bible stated approximately 3,500 years ago in the Book of Genesis.

In the book of Isaiah we read, "*It is* He who sits above the circle of the earth, And its inhabitants *are* like grasshoppers, Who stretches out the heavens like a curtain, And spreads them out like a tent to dwell in." (Isa. 40:22).

For thousands of years, man believed the earth to be flat (Some, called flat earthers, still do). Yet, approximately 2700 years ago the prophet Isaiah, inspired by God wrote that the earth was a circle. Today, modern science has proven in many ways that the earth is a circle. Some, including a small group of Christians, say that the verse in Isaiah means that the earth is a circle but still flat, just as a coin would be a circle but lay flat on one side.

However, scientists have proven that the earth is not circular and flat as a coin laying on its side but the earth spherical. Today this is very easily verified by viewing photos of the earth from outer space. Again, we have an example of science verifying the authenticity of the Bible. The prophet Isaiah couldn't possibly have known this other than from divine revelation from God as there was limited scientific knowledge at the time and no modern scientific instruments.

Isaiah 42:5 reads, "Thus says God the Lord, Who created the heavens and stretched them out, Who spread forth the earth and that which comes from it, Who gives breath to the people on it, And spirit to those who walk on it."

The first part of this verse makes it clear that the universe is expanding. However, there are almost a dozen verses in the Old Testament that show that the universe is expanding and continues to expand (e.g., Job 9:8; Ps. 104:2; Isa. 40:22, Jer. 10:12; Zech. 12:1). Psalm 104:2 and Isaiah 40:22 actually describe the universe's continuous expansion as the "Stretching out" of the heavens like a tent being unfurled. It wasn't until sometime in the 20th century before any other book, whether science, theology, or philosophy, gave the smaller inkling of the universe expanding. Today, with high powered telescopes like the TEC Telescope and Hubble Space Telescope, scientists have confirmed that the universe have been expanding without interruption and continues to do so.

Jeremiah 33:25 says, "This is what the Lord says: 'If My covenant for day and night does not continue, and I have not established the fixed patterns of heaven and earth." (NASB).

By "Fixed patterns of heaven and earth," God is telling us that the laws He has governing the universe are fixed or constant. These laws are what we call scientific laws or laws of physics. Several other Scriptures attest to this, including Gen. 1-3; Eccles. 1:4-11; Rom. 8:18-23). Scientist, using high tech equipment and instruments have made measurements from varying distances from earth and showed the laws of physics have remained constant throughout cosmic history.

Paul wrote to the Romans that "… The creation was subjected to futility, not willingly, but because of Him who subjected *it* in hope; because the creation itself also will be delivered from the bondage of corruption into the glorious liberty of the children of God. For we know that the whole creation groans and labors with birth pangs together until now." (Rom. 8:20-22).

Among other information, we learn from these verses that the universe is decaying and wearing down. Scientists now know this to be a fact through observation and refer to it as the second law of thermodynamics or law of entropy. How could Paul have known this?

We read in the Scriptures, "And the Lord God formed man *of* the dust of the ground, and breathed into his nostrils the breath of life; and man became a living being." (Gen. 2:7).

This verse clearly tells us that the body of a human is composed of what's in the earth. Modern science tells us that human cells are 65-90% water so oxygen contributes the majority of human body mass. The rest of the body is composed of hydrogen, nitrogen, calcium, and phosphorus, all of which are found in the earth's crust.

There are several other such examples that we can cite in the Bible that scientists later discovered, thereby confirming the authenticity of the Scriptures. When the Bible and science indicate disagreements, it is not the Bible and science that disagree (God is the author of both) but it's the *theologians* and/or *scientists* that disagree when they misinterpret or reach wrong conclusions from scientific tests and Bible research.

Testimony of Jesus

Jesus confirmed that He is the Son of God and God the Son by fulfilling the Old Testament prophecies about His coming (Zach. 13:7; John 14:9); performing miracles (Isa. 35:4-6; Matt. 11:4-5, 12:10-13); and predicting and accomplishing His own resurrection (Matt. 28:6). Therefore, as God, Jesus cannot lie (Heb. 6:18) and what He confirmed about the Bible is true. What Jesus testified about the Scriptures referred to the Old Testament because the New Testament was not written until after Jesus had ascended back to heaven.

When we review the teachings of Jesus, we see that Jesus affirmed that the Old Testament is the Word of God (Matt. 15:3, 6); imperishable (Matt. 5:17-18), infallible (John 10:35), inerrant (Matt. 22:29), and true (John 17:17). There are other ways Jesus affirmed the Old Testament to be the Word of God but the verses cited above provide sufficient evidence for the authenticity of the Old Testament. And we have provided evidence above for the authenticity of the New Testament.

What Does it all Mean?

Once we know that the Bible is the true, inerrant, infallible Word of God, then what the Bible says is true, inerrant, and infallible. Thus, when the Bible claims that all knowledge and all wisdom is found in Jesus Christ (Col. 2:2-3), this also means that all knowledge and wisdom is found in the Bible. This is because the Bible is the Word of God and Jesus is the Word of God (2 Tim. 3:16; John 1:1,14) - Jesus the living Word and the Bible, the written Word.

And when Jesus teaches us to live by every Word that comes out of the mouth of God (Matt. 4:4), this means that we are to go to the Bible for all knowledge and wisdom on everything, including on *Race, Racism, and Slavery*.

Race, racism, and slavery involve moral ramifications and must be considered as such. And since the Bible is the foundation for moral principles, we should go to the Bible when addressing these issues. In doing this, because we have the right source, we will never worry about having the wrong perspective, other than perhaps questions in interpretation. When we have differences in interpretation, we prayerfully and lovingly discuss and reason with each other to get the right perspective (Isa. 1:18). Then we agree to adhere to what truth the Holy Spirit enlightens us with, regardless of prior teachings, opinions, or feelings. This is how we let this mind be in us which is also in Christ Jesus (Phil. 2:5).

To determine what is right from what is wrong, there must be a standard with which we human beings must be guided. The standard by which we must be guided must not and cannot change as a changing standard is not a valid standard.

Suppose you were driving on a two-lane highway and came to a red light with another car in the lane beside you that stopped at the red light also. As you both waited for the light to change, you felt as if your car was moving forward so you looked up but the light was still red. The next step you would take is to look to the car beside you to see if it is moving. If it is not moving and yours is, and you looked to see that the light is still red, you know that something is wrong, perhaps you didn't pressed your foot on the brakes sufficiently or the brakes aren't functioning properly.

You know that you're doing something wrong, or something is wrong with your car because you used the car besides you as a standard of measurement. If there were no car beside you and the same situation occurred, you would look for a tree, a fire hydrant, a building or anything else stable or unmoving to determine if you are right or wrong. But suppose the tree or fire hydrant, building or whatever else you looked at was moving. Then your "Standard" is moving and it would no longer be a valid standard to you. It would no longer be helpful to you, and you would have no way of knowing whether you are in the right or wrong because there is no valid standard to use.

This is true for us a human beings in other areas of our lives so God gave us a standard to guide us and one in which we should abide; a standard that would let us know if we are right or wrong in every aspect of our lives – one that does not change, as God does not change (Mal. 3:6; Heb. 13:8). That standard is the Holy Bible which, as shown above, has a perspective (Standard) on everything since this is where all wisdom and knowledge is found. To apply the Bible accurately and sufficiently to *Race, Racism, and Slavery*, there are certain moral foundations that we must possess and apply. The five basic moral foundations that we must always use in making this application are found in the discipline of Christian ethics; and are Love, Justice, Honesty, Integrity, and Civility.[16] At a minimum we must have and use these moral virtues to effectively apply the principles of the Bible to any given situation and/or circumstance.

1. Love - Matt. 22:37-40 – Since God is love and is teaching us to love, when we represent Him we must always represent Him in love. When we apply the Word of God we must do it with love for God first, then our fellowman. To do this any other way would be blasphemy against God and disrespect to our fellowman as well as ourselves.

---

[16] Kerby Anderson, *Christian Ethics in Plain Language*, 27-33.

2. Justice (Job 29:12-17, Ps. 146:7-9, Mal 3:5) – We must always be just in applying the Word of God to various situations and circumstances that we incur in life. Situations that are just and unjust necessitates just application of the Scriptures for a proper biblical response and solution.

3. Honesty (Heb. 13:18) – Like other godly virtues, honesty is critically important when we want to get the biblical perspective. We see dishonesty today in virtually every aspect of life, particularly in politics, entertainment, business, and even among Christian brethren. This should never be if we desire to see everything from a biblical perspective.

4. Integrity (Prov. 11:3; 10:9). The word integrity comes from the same Latin root as integer and implies a wholeness of a person. A person with integrity is a whole person and not divided. This means that the person is not one way today and another way tomorrow. It means that the person doesn't change his or her personality because the situation and circumstances change.

5. Civility (Matt. 22:39) - Being civil means to be polite and courteous in what we say and do around others. It means that we are to abide by certain rules that govern a group, organization, society, business, etc. The rules that are established should be based on the moral laws found in the Scriptures.

Unless we apply these moral foundations each time we attempt to apply biblical principles to any given set of problems, situations, and/or circumstances we will not arrive at the response or conclusion that God wants us to have, meaning we will not be on one accord and in His will.

CHAPTER 2
GOD'S DIVERSITY IN CREATION

After these things I looked, and behold, a great multitude which no one could number, of all nations, tribes, peoples, and tongues, standing before the throne and before the Lamb, clothed with white robes, with palm branches in their hands (Rev. 7:9).

Diversity in the Trinity

The Bible shows us that our Creator God is Triune. The Triune or Trinity nature of God is reflected in the diversity in His creation. So, we believe it may be helpful to provide some foundational information about the Trinity, as this can help us in understanding why God has such a great love for diversity. One of the greatest doctrines in the Christian faith is that of the Triune God, and it is one of the most difficult doctrines to understand. It's difficulty in understanding is sometimes compared to our understanding of the Virgin birth and resurrection but because we cannot fully understand it, does not mean we should disregard it as being untrue. We must always believe what the Bible teaches regardless of our understanding. For example, we can't understand how God can create something out of nothing but the Bible clearly says this is what happened (Gen. 1:1; Col. 1:16) and here we are.

From our studies and research, we have been made aware that Christianity is the only religion in world that believes and teaches the doctrine of the Trinity. There is no other major world religion that sees God as a Triune God. Furthermore, even out of the more than 3,000 Christian cults in the United States, we know of none that teaches or sees God as Triune. The doctrine of the Trinity is difficult to understand and perhaps even more difficult to explain. Yet, it is important to understand diversity and unity in God's nature.

But just what do we mean when we say that God is a Trinity? Simply stated, we mean that there is one God but there are three eternally distinct persons within that Godhead. When we say that there is one God in three distinct persons, we mean that God is one in essence (being or nature) and three in persons.

We know from the Scriptures that there is only one God (Deut. 6:4; 1 Tim. 2:5). Yet the Bible tells us that the Father is God (John 6:27; Rom 1:7); the Son is God (John 1:1,16; Col 2:9); and the Holy Spirit is God (Acts 5:3-4). So, we see that the Bible makes it clear that there is one God but three persons in the Godhead, the Father is God, the Son is God, and the Holy Spirit is God. We understand that each, the Father, Son, and Holy Spirit is a person because it takes three characteristics to be a person: mind, emotion, and will. The Bible shows that God the Father has all three, God the Son has all three, and God the Holy Spirit has all three, so all three in the Trinity are indeed separate, distinct persons. One reason why so many Christians do not believe in the Trinity is because there have been few attempts to explain and understand it, and many of the explanations are confusing or contain contradictions.

For example, some say that the Trinity is like water, which has three states – solid, liquid, and gas. One portion of water, say one quart, can exist in all three stages. The problem with this illustration is that water is not solid, liquid, or gas at the same time.

But God is Father, Son, and Holy Spirit at the same time, while still being one God. Therefore, this is not a good illustration of the Trinity. Another bad illustration is that the Trinity is like a three-link chain. There is only one chain but the chain has three links to it. The problem here is that the links are three different items, whereas God is one and not three. Another illustration is that God is like a man who is composed of spirit, soul, and body.

Every human being is one person, yet each is composed of spirit, soul, and body. The problem with this analogy is that the spirit and soul separate from the body at death, but the members of the Godhead are inseparable. There are problems with each of these examples but there are other good illustrations such as a person's mind, ideas, and words, or one to the third power, or love which involves a lover, a beloved, and a spirit of love. But one that I've found to be really helpful and maybe the most valid illustration of the Trinity would be that of a Triangle.

The triangle is one figure but has three different sides or corners at the same time, so there is a simultaneous threeness and oneness and this doesn't violate any of the principles as do the others. There is the Father, Son, and Holy Spirit. Each one is a separate distinct person and they all existed together for all eternity, yet all are God – all have a divine nature. The Father is not the Son or Holy Spirit. The Son is not the Father or Holy Spirit, and the Holy Spirit is not the Father or Son. This view, called modalism is what some Christian denominations believe; that the Father, Son, and Holy Spirit are only different in "modes" rather than being three eternally distinct persons. As we've seen above, this view is not biblical. Also, the unbiblical view is the view that there are three separate Gods, as some Christian cults believe, which is called tritheism. One of the doctrines that the Bible repeatedly makes abundantly clear is that there is only one God.

Some Christians say, wait a minute, the word trinity isn't found in the Bible. This is true but the word itself doesn't have to be found in the Bible as long as the word properly captures the *truth* that is found in the Bible. In theology, we use many words that are not found in the Bible but accurately reflect biblical truth.

For example, the word atheism is not found in the Bible but we use it frequently to identify those who do not believe in God. The word divinity is not found in the Bible yet it is used thousands of times or more each day to refer to God and His nature. The word rapture is not found in the Bible, but it is used somewhere daily by those who believe and those who do not believe in the doctrine of the rapture, either to confirm or deny it. Or consider, this: Even the word Bible isn't found in the Bible but when we say "Holy Bible" as people do every day, everyone knows precisely what is meant.

The point we are making here is that we can coin a phrase or word as long as that word accurately describes the biblical doctrine, event, or phenomenon and sticks to the truth. It just so happens that the word Trinity was coined by early church father Tertullian in 160 AD so you can see that this was not a term invented by the current church, but it has been used for 2,000 years. Now what kind of relationship did the Father, Son, and Holy Spirit have? The Father, Son, and Holy Spirit have existed together in this relationship in perfect love for all eternity. The Father has always been the Father, Jesus has always been the Son, and the Holy Spirit has always been the third person of the Triune God. This is the true nature of God – diversity in the Godhead yet unity as one God. So, because there is diversity in the unity of the Trinity, we know that it is a part of God's nature and that God loves diversity.

So, now we see that there is diversity in the Godhead, the Trinity. However, there is also diversity in the Second Person of the Godhead, Jesus Christ. Jesus is the only one of the Godhead that has two natures. He has a human nature and a divine nature. The human nature is not the same as divine nature and is not integrated or a part of His divine nature. This is why when we ask a question of Jesus, we have to ask it twice, one of His divine nature and one of His human nature. Did Jesus get hungry? In His divine nature, no; in His human nature, yes. Did Jesus get tired? In His divine nature, no, in His human nature, yes. Did Jesus get sleepy? In His divine nature, no. In His human nature, yes. Could Jesus die? In His divine nature, no; in His human nature, yes.

This is important to understand about Jesus' dual nature and is referred to in theology as the hypostatic union. This has been a stumbling block to many Christians and world religions because, since they don't understand it, they refuse to believe. However, the Bible makes it abundantly clear that Jesus is God and man. We know that Jesus is God (Col. 2:9). As God He cannot change (Mal 3:6; Heb. 13:8). Yet He became a man (John 1:1-3; 14). Since He is God and cannot change, yet He became a man, in order to complete the hypostatic union, He had to have added humanity to His deity – thus the God-man. So again, we see diversity not only in the Godhead but also in the Second Person of the Godhead.

We even see God's love for diversity in His Word, the Holy Bible. Consider just these five facts about the Bible:

1. The Bible was written by approximately 40 people, men, and women, of different backgrounds.
2. The Bible was written on three different continents (Modern day Africa, Asia, and Europe).

3. The Bible was written in three different languages (Hebrew, Greek, and Aramaic).
4. The Bible contains two Testaments, Old, and New.
5. The Bible contains 66 books, 39 in Old Testament, 27 in New Testament.

God could've used one person on one continent to write one book in one language and that would've been the end of it. God certainly has His divine reasons for getting His word out to man in the manner in which He did but one thing that we know with certain from this: God loves diversity.

Diversity in the Church

Jesus said I will build my church and the gates of hades will not prevail against it (Matt. 16:18). Jesus was making it clear to His disciples that no one could destroy His church and the church would be around forever, until He returns to get it. And noticed how He structured His church:

"And He Himself gave some *to be* apostles, some prophets, some evangelists, and some pastors and teachers, for the equipping of the saints for the work of ministry, for the edifying of the body of Christ, till we all come to the unity of the faith and of the knowledge of the Son of God, to a perfect man, to the measure of the stature of the fullness of Christ." (Ephes. 4:11-13).

God placed different categories of leadership to oversee and run the church to accomplish one of His purposes of edifying the saints. The other two primary purposes for the church are to worship and glorify God (John 4:23) and get the gospel out to the world (Matt. 28:19).

We will give more information on the purpose of the church in Chapter 8 but here, we even see diversity in God's purposes for the church. In the verses in Ephesians Chapter 4, Paul emphasizes that God appointed different positions to "Come to the unity of the faith and of the knowledge of the Son of God" to help us all come into the fullness of Christ. He's using diversity to bring us into unity with Him. Diversity is important to God, and He loves diversity. So, in His creation, He extended this diverse pattern to His creation. With careful observation, we see that the entire cosmos and everything else in creation displays diversity.

Consider the number of stars in the universe. It is estimated that the Milky Way Galaxy has between 100 and 400 billion stars. There are more than 100 billion galaxies in the universe with some researchers placing the figure at about 500 billion. According to World Atlas Website, there are four types of galaxies: elliptical, spiral, barred spiral, and irregular. Most of these galaxies are between 1 to 100 parsecs away and 3 to 300 light-years in diameter. It was once estimated that there were 200 billion galaxies but now the number of known galaxies is believed to be 2 trillion. The lowest number of stars that can be found in the universe is ten sextillions (10 billion billion).[17]

These stars have a variety of sizes, shapes, and life spans which demonstrates some of God's diversity in the cosmos. And to show the awesomeness of God the Bible says He knows all of these stars and calls them all by name! (Psalm 147:4). Also, in our Milky Way Galaxy, there are nine planets but when we consider the other galaxies, scientists estimate that there are at least 100 billion planets.

Even falling snowflakes are different and as we've learned in our science classes in school, no two snowflakes are the same. Of course, we are aware that on the macroscopic scale, two or more

[17] *https://www.nasa.gov/topics/universe/features/micro20120111.html*

snowflakes can appear identical in shapes and sizes but on a molecular and atomic level, all of these snowflakes differ in terms of the number of atoms and isotopic ration, which is created by God.

God also made man in His own image and there is diversity in man as we shall see later in this Chapter but there is also diversity in the angelic realm, the animal kingdom, and the plant kingdom.

Diversity in the Angelic Realm

The Bible tells us that God created angels (Psalm 148:2-5) and while we do not know how many angels there are, we know that angels are associated with stars in the Bible (Job 38:7; Rev. 9:1-2) and as mentioned above, the number of stars in the universe is estimated to be at least ten sextillions (10 billion billion). Daniel, speaking of God, says that "Thousands upon thousands attended him; ten thousands times ten thousand stood before him" (Dan. 7:10). John in Revelation said, "Then I looked and heard the voice of many angels, numbering thousands upon thousands, and ten thousand times ten thousand." (Rev. 5:11).

Notice that John said he heard angels "Numbering thousands upon thousands *and* ten thousand times ten thousands." This is 100 million in addition to the thousands upon thousands. Based on this information, we can be reasonably certain that angels number in the billions or even trillions. This itself shows that God is a God of diversity because the Bible shows that all angels are not the same and God has classification with names for each, while individually naming some in the Bible. There are different ranks of angels. For example, we see that angels are ranked as rulers, principalities, powers, thrones, and dominions (Col. 2:10; 1 Peter 3:22; Eph. 1:20-21). Beyond these, God also categorized the angels with diverse levels of authority, including archangel Michael, the cherubim, the seraphim, and Gabriel. *Talk about diversity?*

Diversity in the Animal Kingdom

Most of us are aware that God told Noah to put two males and females of every living animal on the ark (Gen. 6:19-20). But not many of us consider additional instructions God gave Noah about animals to go on the ark.

"You shall take with you seven each of every clean animal, a male and his female; two each of animals that are unclean, a male and his female; 3 also seven each of birds of the air, male and female, to keep the species alive on the face of all the earth." (Gen. 7:2-3).

In other words, God told Noah that while selecting "Two" of every kind of animal on the ark, when it came to clean animals (Clean animals are those that chew the cud and part the hoof, clean fish have fins and scales, and clean birds are those that do not eat carrion and have other forbidden characteristics (see Lev. 11 and Deut. 14:11-18)) to bring seven pairs of male and female.

When it came to unclean animals, he was to bring in one pair, male and female. Then seven pairs of every kind of birds, male and female. God did this to keep the various species alive on earth, again showing His love for diversity. But it didn't stop there. God obviously programmed Deoxyribonucleic Acid (DNA) in these animals to enable them to have diverse offspring as every species of animal was not brought onto the ark. Yet, today we have millions of species of various land animals, sea animals, and animals that fly. In fact, God has created hundreds of millions of different life-forms.[18]

Consider land animals for example, specifically the different breeds of dogs. While Noah may have placed two dogs in the ark, today the American Kennel Club (AKC) recognizes more than 200 breeds! This includes terriers, hounds, shepherds, collies, etc. With cats, the International Cat Association recognizes 71 standardized breeds which is less than AKC with dogs but considerably more than the two that Noah brought on the ark.

God even made animals different in such a way as to be a blessing to man in various capacities. Some animals were made to be domesticated for agricultural, farming, or ranching purposes (e.g., horses, donkeys, cows, sheep, goats). Others were domesticated to be pets (e.g., dogs, cats, rabbits, hamsters). If we watch little children interact with animals, you will immediately see the strong, powerful desire to relate from both sides, child and animal. These animals were created with intelligence, emotions, and instinct that enable them to relate with humans.

We're all familiar with various forms of sea life like sharks, whales, dolphins, seals, sea lions, various fish, etc. But according to the Smithsonian Website, there are over 17,000 species of marine life in the sea. A study was conducted by the Census of Marine Life, over a 10-year period to assess the diversity (How many different kinds), distribution (Where they live), and abundance (How many individuals) of marine life. This research included approximately 2,700 scientists from more than 80 countries. The scope of the Census of Marine Life inspired a variety of authors and artists to tell this story through films and

---

[18] Hugh Ross, *Why the Universe is the Way it is*; 186.

writings.[19] Again, we see examples of God's love for diversity in which man is still discovering. However, while we continue to discover God's diversity, we certainly have enough today to confirm that God is the God of diversity.

These are just examples to show God's diversity but consider this as well. God made antelopes, elephants, hippopotamus, rhinoceros, lions, bears, giraffes, gorillas, hogs, snakes, chickens, ducks, eagles, turtles, sharks, alligators, whales, butterflies, mosquitoes, zebras, hyenas, snails, shrimps, octopus, seals, mice, kangaroos, frogs, and hundreds of thousands of other different breeds and types of animals and insects – all with different sizes, shapes, and other characteristics. Some have two feet, some have four. Some have wings, others do not. Some have fins or flippers, others do not. Some live in shells, others do not. Some lay eggs, others carry their young – awesome love for diversity found in our Creator!

Diversity Among Insects

Most people know that there seem to be multiple billions of insects around but when it comes to the difference in species or types of insects, that is another story. Scientists tell us that there are some 900 thousand different kinds of living insects known, but there are more unknown than those that are known. Consider this statement from the Smithsonian Institute's Website:

"In the United States, the number of described species is approximately 91,000. The undescribed species of insects in the United States, however, is estimated at some 73,000. The largest numbers of described species in the U.S. fall into four insect Orders: Coleoptera (beetles) at 23,700, Diptera (flies) at 19,600,

---

[19] *The Census of Marine Life | Smithsonian Ocean (si.edu)*

Hymenoptera (ants, bees, wasps) at 17,500, and Lepidoptera (moths and butterflies) at 11,500."[20]

God created the world and everything in it (Acts 17:24) and the mere fact that He took time to create thousands and millions of species and types for something that we look at as insignificant as insects shows His great love for diversity.

Diversity in the Plant Kingdom

There are hundreds of thousands of plants in the plant kingdom. With just flowers alone, there are over 400,000 different types with different shapes, color combinations, odor, and other distinctions. These include the more familiar ones we know as roses, azaleas, daisies, daffodils, carnations, tulips, sunflowers, orchids, lilacs, and many others. All very beautiful – God loves variety.

Then there are millions of other types of plants that are so different that they are widely used for different purposes in our livelihood. Plants are used for clothing, furniture, pesticides, medicine, rubber, shelter, prevent soil erosions, and many other purposes.

Diversity in Humans

Human beings are the last of God's creation and as we've seen, He has used diversity in every aspect of His creation. It follows then that He would have diversity in the creation of human beings. Right after creating the first man, He said that "It is not good that the man should be alone, I will make him a helper comparable to him." (Gen. 2:18). He then placed the man into a deep sleep, took a rib from his body, and created the woman. Then

---

[20] *https://www.si.edu/spotlight/buginfo/bugno*

He brought them together in a marriage ceremony and told them to go forth, have children and replenish the earth (Gen. 1:28).

Some sources have estimated that from the time of Adam and Eve to the present, there have been approximately 108 billion people that lived on the earth. That is a tremendous amount of people but what is even more fascinating about this is that no two human beings are exactly alike, including identical twins. While there are environmental and social factors contributing to differences in various human beings, this does not account for the original differences as designed by God. For example, every human being has different fingerprints and eye patterns. There are different shapes of noses, mouths, ears, foreheads, chins, etc. - all resulting from different DNA designed by God. We will address the DNA and race factor in Chapter 3.

In the meantime, why is it that God loves diversity? Is there a specific purpose for human beings created differently? We know that one of the many attributes of God is love and that God is love (1 John 4:7-8). We also know that God is conforming us into the image of His Son (Rom. 8:29). To help in accomplishing this God created the universe in such a way that would facilitate this process. By having diversity in His creation, it helps us to develop an appreciation for beauty as we see the different aspects of His creation. For example, some will see the beauty in a rose, while others will see the beauty in violets, lilies, or daffodils. Some will see the beauty in a Cocker Spaniel, while other fall in love with a Poodle, husky or German Shepherd. It is the variety that first catches the eye and makes them more appealing. In other words, one of the reasons we learn to love and appreciate these flowers and animals is because they are different.

Now think about the differences in human beings. While we are all created in the image of God, we are all different in our physical appearance. People are tall, short, stocky, slim, dark skin, light-skin, different shape noses, mouths, eyes, and ears. Then there are differences in cultures, and activities we pursue for business and pleasure, and many other differences for which we can point. Now once God gets us to love people that are different from we are, then we have made significant growth towards becoming more like Jesus. This is not as easy as one might think because it is human nature to tease and ridicule others who are different. The enemy uses these differences to inspire various groups of people to say, "We're better than they are, they are not like us." The enemy also uses our differences to start different "races" and cause division. As you read through the rest of this book, you will see a significant number of problems, including death brought about by human beings because of differences, just the opposite of what God wants us to accomplish.

CHAPTER 3
WHAT MAKE HUMANS DIFFERENT

And He has made from one blood every nation of men to dwell on all the face of the earth, and has determined their preappointed times and the boundaries of their dwellings, (Acts 17:26).

How Different Are We?

Racial problems have existed from the early part of creation as men sought to flaunt their superiority over other men as a result of skin color and other physical characteristics. We've seen in Chapter 2 how we are different physically from an external perspective but just how different is one human being from another internally, when we get to the internal, physical parts of our being?

As stated in verse above, The Apostle Paul told the Athenians that we all came from one blood so just how different can we be? One scientific study concluded that the DNA of any two people would differ by only 2/10ths of one percent. Furthermore, of this very slight difference, only six percent can be linked to any racial categories. The other 94% making up this difference is within race variation.[21] Stated differently, from a scientific viewpoint, all of these racial differences that man has been using to distinguish himself as superior to other men are statistically insignificant. This

---

[21] Kirby Anderson, *Christian Ethics in Plain Language.* 174.

confirms what Paul said to the Athenians about coming from one blood.

What is Race?

Generally, when we think of "race," we think of skin color, hair texture, facial features, and other physical characteristics. However, these distinctions are social attributes as race is not a biological or scientific classification. "Race" is a manmade term or human concept and has nothing to do with physiological characteristics. Physical features like eye color, skin color, hair features can be found across racial lines. For example, we can find dark skin Africans with blue eyes and very straight hair. Or we can find Caucasians with curly hair and darker skin. It is true however, that these traits are more common in some groups than others, but they cannot be used as identifying factors for specific racial groups.

Consider the following statement made from the American Anthropological Association:

Skin color varies largely from light in the temperate areas in the north to dark in the tropical areas in the south; its intensity is not related to nose shape or hair texture. Dark skin may be associated with frizzy or kinky hair or curly or wavy or straight hair, all of which are found among different indigenous people in tropical regions. These facts render any attempt to establish lines of division among biological populations both arbitrary and subjective.[22]

This is supported by DNA testing as stated above. Modern science has confirmed that we are too biologically similar to

---

[22] *American Anthropological Association Statement on "Race"*, May 17, 1998.

provide any objective distinguishing physiological features by racial groups.

The American Anthropological Association Report continued:

Historical research has shown that the idea of "race" has always carried more meanings than mere physical differences; indeed, physical variations in the human species have no meaning except the social ones that humans put on them. Today, scholars in many fields argue that "race" as it is understood in the United States of America was a social mechanism invented during the 18th century to refer to those populations brought together in colonial America: the English and other European settlers, the conquered Indian peoples, and those peoples of Africa brought in to provide slave labor. [23]

As we've seen, race is not relegated to physical or biological features in human beings. However, this does not mean that there aren't any differences in human beings; but these differences are attributed to other factors as explained below.

Ethnic and Cultural Differences

There are obvious cultural differences as they are clearly and more frequently seen by more people with the increase in advanced technology and travel. These cultural differences usually affect how we talk, eat, sing, listen to music, worship, and various other aspects of our lives. Blacks may generally prefer different music than whites. Whites may prefer different types of food than Blacks, or both groups may even prefer different types of sports or entertainment, but these are cultural traits or preferences which are taught and not inherent from race.

---

[23] Ibid.

The American Anthropological Association Report also confirmed this in their findings.

At the end of the 20th century, we now understand that human cultural behavior is learned, conditioned into infants beginning at birth, and always subject to modification. No human is born with a built-in culture or language. Our temperaments, dispositions, and personalities, regardless of genetic propensities, are developed within sets of meanings and values that we call "Culture." Studies of infant and early childhood learning, and behavior attest to the reality of our cultures in forming who we are.[24]

When black babies or infants are adopted and raised by white parents, in each case that black child grew up talking and using mannerisms as its white adoptive parents; and listening to the same type of music she heard when she was brought up.

But even though race is not biological or scientific, racial distinctions permeate virtually every part of our society. We're reminded of this for example, when an application or other document which is required to be completed for a job or other position contains questions as to whether the applicant is White American, Black or African American, Native American, Alaska Native, Asian American, Native Hawaiian, Other Pacific Islander; White Spanish, Black Spanish or a number of other racial categories which seem to be growing with each generation.

Furthermore, race is used as a barometer to determine who gets accepted to various educational and social institutions, who receive government scholarships and grants, who are accepted in housing projects, etc. In today's culture, it doesn't matter that some

---

[24] Ibid.

of these practices are illegal, for in many cases, the law is ignored where race is involved.

For example, a recent COVID-19 bill included funds to be distributed to American farmers but only to minority farmers. A black farmer who is facing no hardships and doing well financially will receive funds while a white farmer who is struggling financially gets nothing. While those governmental officials implementing these laws and policies in all probability mean well, this is not racial justice but racial injustice. This is more and more prevalent in our society today and no longer just whites against blacks, but the tables have been turned where in many cases, blacks are given favor over whites. We will have more to say on this later, but decisions based on race is prominent in many areas of our lives today. In fact, in America, decisions based on race apparently are ingrained in our culture socially, economically, environmentally, psychologically, politically, and many other ways.

Skin Tone Differences

First, it should be noted that there is strong evidence that all human life began in Africa. Biblical evidence and scientific evidence are consistent in verifying that human life, not just black life but all human life originated in Africa. For example, when we go to the Bible, we see a description of the Garden of Eden which helps us in determining its possible location. Notice what the Bible says in Genesis:

[10] Now a river went out of Eden to water the garden, and from there it parted and became four riverheads. [11] The name of the first *is* Pishon; it *is* the one which skirts the whole land of Havilah, where *there is* gold. [12] And the gold of that land *is* good. Bdellium and the onyx stone *are* there. [13] The name of the second

river *is* Gihon; it *is* the one which goes around the whole land of Cush. [14] The name of the third river *is* Hiddekel; it *is* the one which goes toward the east of Assyria. The fourth river *is* the Euphrates (Gen. 2:10-14).

According to this passage, the Rivers Pishon and Gihon are closely associated with Cush. Cush is present-day Ethiopia, Southern Egypt, and Sudan in Africa and the River Gihon winds through the entire nation of Cush. This geographic description alone provides strong evidence that the Garden of Eden's location is in Africa.

Some believe that because of the flood during the time of Noah, we can't know if the rivers are in the same location as they were before the flood. This is a reasonable consideration. However, we must remember that when Moses wrote the book of Genesis (Between 1527 and 1487 BC)[25] the flood had already taken place, so the description of the location was spoken of in the present tense.

The Dean of Howard University's School of Divinity, Dr. Cain Hope Felder, stated the following:

"Clearly, wherever else 'Eden' extended its beginning was within the continent of Africa." [26]

Furthermore, Dr. Edwin Yamauchi, professor emeritus of history at Miami University Ohio and author of *Africa and the Bible,* stated that the majority of scholars identify the Gihon River with the Nile, which ran through the land of Cush.[27] While this may not be generally known and widely publicized, the consensus

---

[25] Norman L. Geisler, *A Popular Survey of the Old Testament,* 36.
[26] H. C. Felder, *The African American Guide to the Bible*, 145.
[27] Ibid.

among most of the scientific community today is that all of human life originated in Africa. Notice the following from an article on *The Story of Africa* by the BBC, "So far the evidence that we have in the world points to Africa as the Cradle of Humankind."[28] This is based on fossil identification, radiocarbon dating, and DNA analysis.

In addition to this, the idea that the Garden of Eden was in Africa would also correspond with the scientific evidence that human life started in Africa.

According to an article in *Scientific American Magazine,* "Humans left Africa and gradually fanned out across Asia to Australia and then up to Europe; and then say 15,000 years ago, they crossed over what was then a land bridge to the Americans and gradually worked their way down to South America."[29]

An Article by *CNN* says, "Advanced DNA testing, combined with recently unearthed discoveries are bolstering the belief that if you look back far enough, all living human beings are the descendants of a small, innovative and ambitions set of people on the African continent." [30]

The overall consensus is that after the first human beings started in Africa, they grew and spread from that area to other parts of the world. This populated the entire world and, in that sense, all human beings are Africans. All of this means that anyone alive today can trace his or her roots back to Africa, regardless of their present color or race. This also means that a white European can

---

[28] Ibid. 124.
[29] Ibid.
[30] Ibid.

literally trace his ancestry to people who are as dark as the average African American.

"Rather than seeing Europeans and Asians as 'races,' they may be more accurately seen as different-looking subsets of Africans, since the human population descended from human beings living on the continent."[31]

The obvious question at this point would be, "If we're all from the African continent, why are we so different in skin colors, black, white, brown, etc.?" There are four factors that account for these differences:

1. Deoxyribonucleic Acid (DNA)
2. Ultra-Violet Radiation (UVR) – Electromagnetic radiation or light from the sun.
3. Vitamin D – Associated with the amount of ultraviolet radiation we receive from the sun.
4. Melanin – A dark pigment responsible for tanning of skin exposed to sunlight.

The difference in our skin colors results from our need for Vitamin D and where we are geographically located on the globe. When God created mankind, He created us with a need for Vitamin D. The medical industry has provided us with a wealth of information on the importance of Vitamin D for the health of the human body.

For example, Vitamin D is needed to strengthen our bones and muscles, support the immune system, fight inflammation, help strengthen oral health, help prevent type 1 and 2 diabetes, help treat hypertension, help battle depression, and even help lose

---

[31] Ibid. 126.

weight. In short, Vitamin D is necessary for a healthy life and human life period.

The vast majority of Vitamin D we receive comes from the sun and our bodies have been programmed to convert UVRs from the sun into Vitamin D. These UVRs enter our bodies through our skin and our skin tone determines how much Vitamin D is absorbed. In other words, our skin tone regulates the amount of Vitamin D that enters our bodies.

Differences in skin color come about as our bodies attempt to strike a balance in our need for Vitamin D and to protect ourselves from harmful rays of the sun. To help in this process, God supplied the body with melanin. Melanin is a dark pigment in the skin that tans the skin when it is exposed to sunlight. When life began in Africa and generations began to form, all people had skin colors of different shades of brown (Remember God's love for diversity in Chapter 2).

As we remember from elementary school, the equator is an imaginary line drawn around the earth equally distant from both poles, dividing the earth into northern and southern hemispheres. There were no "white" people as we know of today. But as people migrated away from the equator, they developed lighter skin (microevolution) in order to allow more Vitamin D into their bodies. This is because the further one moves from the equator, the level of UVRs hitting earth's surface decreases due to the earth's tilt at approximately 23 degrees. UVRs hit the equator all year round but because of the tilt of the earth and seasonal variations, people in Northern Europe receive much less UVR exposure in winters. This means their skins would have to lighten up to absorb sufficient UVRs.

Over thousands of years, skin tones adapted to meet the needs of the people based on the region in which they live. And this is why people in Europe have lighter skin tones or are "white." Those closer to the equator have darker skin tones or are "black." If you look at a skin tone map, you will see these differences immediately (see Figures 3.1 and 3.2).

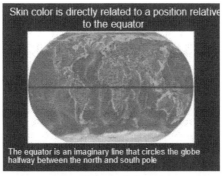

Figure 3.1

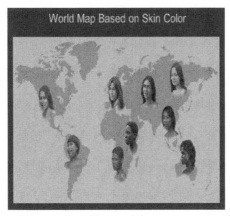

Figure 3.2

The people moving away from the equator developed lighter skin through a process called microevolution. Microevolution is a change in gene frequency within a population in a relatively short period of time, say a generation or so. This is done so that humans (and animals) can more easily adapt to their climate and environment and is programmed in DNA by God.

People moving away from the equator developed lighter skin so that they could absorb more UVRs to make more Vitamin D. Over time, this changed the complexion of the people living there and is naturally passed down to all descendants. This does not mean that the light from the sun is stronger or weaker at the equator, but the light hits the earth at different angles, depending on latitude. At very high latitudes (near the Poles), the light hits at a glancing angle, at lower latitudes (near the equator) the light hits more straight-on. So, the light is more concentrated near the equator and less concentrated near the Poles.

A frequently asked question in this analogy is that if all of this is true about UVRs, Vitamin D, Melanin, and skin tone, what about the Alaskans (Inuits) who are far away from the equator but still have dark skin? This is a great question indeed and has been brought up in Bible study classes by various students as we taught on this subject over the years. The answer is found in the diets of the Alaskan people. The Innuits have a rich diet of Vitamin D from certain seafoods (salmon, herring, cods, tuna, etc.) they consume. Therefore, it is unnecessary for their skin tone to make adjustments to receive Vitamin D from the sun. This is similar to many people who take Vitamin D tablets today. Doctors recommend this for those who are rarely outside in the sunlight.

In summary, skin color adapted over thousands of years to meet the need for Vitamin D. Depending on the regions where people live, the amount of sunlight varies. Melanin in the skin allows darker skin to block dangerous amounts of UVRs while allowing those with lighter skin to absorb healthy amounts of UVRs to make sufficient Vitamin D. Our skin color is mainly related to the amount of melanin in the deeper layers of the skin. How much UVR our bodies absorb is related to the amounts of melanin in our skin. Over time, humans increased their production of melanin to meet the new environmental demand of greater UVRs exposure.[32] For hair and eye color differences, see comments under "What is Race?" in this Chapter.

---

[32] Ibid. 128-129.

CHAPTER 4
THE BIBLICAL PERSPECTIVE

For the word of God is living and powerful, and sharper than any two-edged sword, piercing even to the division of soul and spirit, and of joints and marrow, and is a discerner of the thoughts and intents of the heart (Hebrews 4:12).

Race in the Bible

While we are using the term "race" throughout this book, it is important to know that the Bible does not speak of race in the sense that it is used today. When the term race is used in the Bible, it refers to running or pursuing a particular course. When referring to a category of people the Bible only speaks of one race, the human race. As stated before, race is an imprecise term that has no distinguishing characteristics, like hair texture, skin color, etc. Whites, blacks, Latinos, Asians, Indians, Arabs, Jews are not different races. They are different ethnicities of the human race. Race is not a biblical concept, instead, the Bible deals with people as nations and ethnicities.

Origin and Separation of the Nations

Since God dealt with nations other than races, an understanding of how and why God started the nations would be helpful. This is also helpful since many people today, Christians and non-Christians, use God's separation of the nations as justification for separation of the races. A brief history of the first part of the book of Genesis will help us in forming the background of the origin and separation of the nations.

God created Adam and Eve and gave Adam instructions as to not eat of the tree of knowledge of good and evil (Gen. 2:15-17). Adam and Eve failed the test and sinned, which brought death and judgment on them, and all their descendants (Gen. 3). Their son Cain sinned by killing his brother Abel (Gen. 4:1-8) and started a civilization that eventually became evil. This civilization brought wickedness and violence, which filled the earth and precipitated a flood that killed everyone on earth except 8 people: Noah and his wife, their three sons, and their wives (Gen. 7-8).

In the meantime, God was developing a godly nation of people through Noah to fulfill His promise to bring a Savior into the world (Gen. 3:15). After the flood, God blessed Noah and his sons and commanded them to be fruitful and multiply and fill the earth (Gen. 9:1). Instead of following God's commands to "fill the earth", they gathered in one central location and multiplied. Wanting to establish their own nation, the descendants of Noah, through Ham, developed a wicked kingdom centered around the tower of Babel, which God had to judge by scattering them abroad (Gen. 10-11).

It is important to understand that God scattered the nations to prevent them from unifying without God and establishing a world kingdom motivated by their own vanity. The nations were scattered (separated) to prevent them from establishing a world kingdom without God, not because of race. Also, notice that God was in the process of sending a Savior to enable man to be reconciled to Him. Before these groups of people were scattered, they were one culture, that spoke one language. All of these people were born and raised in the Middle East, Mediterranean part of the earth and were different shades of brown in color. Most Middle Easterners are of this same hue today. At that time, there were no "blacks" or "whites" as we know of today. However, these scattered groups are the foundation for people we identify racially and ethnically today. Genesis 10 is referred to as the "Table of Nations" and shows the world was populated by Noah's descendants. As mentioned in Chapter 3, skin color (Black, white, and various shades in between) came later as the people migrated into Europe, Asia, and other parts of the globe, closer to or farther away from the equator. (Refer to Chapter 3 for more detail on skin color).

Was Ham Cursed?

Some whites have used the Bible to support their views that blacks were cursed through Ham. Ham was one of the three sons of the biblical patriarch Noah, the other two sons being Shem and Japheth (Gen. 9:18-27). The belief that blacks were cursed through Ham has been used to justify slavery, racial discrimination, as well as oppression of blacks. This view is based on the story found in Genesis 9.

The Patriarch Noah had become drunk after drinking wine and laid either naked or partially naked in his tent. Ham, the father of Canaan, saw his father naked and went outside and told his two brothers, Shem and Japheth. All types of outrageous ideas have sprung up from this event and what Ham supposedly did. The Bible Knowledge Commentary of the Old Testament says this:

"The rabbis said Ham castrated Noah, thus explaining why Noah had no other sons. Others claim that Ham slept with his mother, thus uncovering his father's nakedness and that Canaan was the offspring of this union. Others have said that Ham was involved in a homosexual attack on his father. But the Hebrew expression here means what it says: Ham … saw …. his father' nakedness (v. 22)." [33]

So you see the wide array of stories circulating to explain this event. Nevertheless, the story continues where the two brothers, Shem and Japheth, took a garment and covered their father, walking backward as not to view his nakedness. When Noah awoke and discovered what Ham had done, he said, "Cursed be Canaan! The lowest of slaves will he be to his brothers. He also stated, "Blessed *be* the LORD, The God of Shem, And may Canaan be his servant Praise be to the Lord, the God of Shem! May Canaan be the slave of Shem. **27** May God enlarge Japheth, And may he dwell in the tents of Shem; And may Canaan be his servant." (Gen. 9:20-27)

This seems like a rather harsh punishment for something as simple as seeing one's father naked. After all, people see others naked quite commonly in various situations today, especially in families. But this is different, as further explained in the Bible Knowledge Commentary:

"To the ancients, however, even seeing one's father naked was a breach of family ethic. The sanctity of the family was destroyed and the strength of the father was made a mockery. Ham apparently stumbled on this accidentally, but went out and exultingly told his two brothers, as if he had triumphed over his father." [34]

---

[33] John F. Walvoord and Roy B. Zuck; *The Bible Knowledge Commentary, Old Testament*; 41.
[34] Ibid.

From this passage of Scripture, some whites and even some blacks believed that slavery was a consequence of this curse. However, this view is faulty for a variety of reasons.

First, the Bible in no way says or otherwise indicates that God cursed people with black skin. As we've seen in Chapter 3, skin color changed as a result of geographic location in proximity to the equator.

Second, Canaan, Ham's son was cursed, not Ham. So if only one of Ham's four sons was cursed, how could all black people be cursed?

Third, there's no indication in this passage of Scripture or anywhere in the Bible that Noah spoke for God. The Bible does not always approve of what it records (e.g. polygamy, fornication, etc.). Noah may very well have just been speaking out of anger.

Fourth, even if a curse was given to Canaan and his descendants, God places limitations on curses to the third and fourth generations (Exo. 20:5-6).

Fifth, the Bible shows that this prophetic curse by Noah on Canaan was fulfilled during the Jewish occupation of the Promised land; with Israel's defeat of Canaan (Joshua 9:23; 1 Kings 9:20-21).

Sixth, the issue of blacks being cursed didn't come up as a significant factor until the rise of slavery in America. Notice this excerpt from Associate Professor of Religious Studies, Stephen R. Haynes.

"Only with the growth of the slave trade and the increasing reliance of sub-Saharan Africa a source for slaves did the curse's role as a justification for racial slavery eclipse its function as a scriptural explanation of either 'Blackness' in particular or servitude in general." [35]

A serious and honest study of the Scriptures and history would have to conclude that slavery and oppressions of blacks had nothing to do with Noah's curse on Ham.

Some whites believe and have argued that various symbolism in the Bible prove that blacks are cursed. This is because in some areas of the Bible white is associated with good and dark is associated with bad or evil. Therefore, black people are cursed. For example, 2 Samuel 22:29 says, "For You are my lamp, O Lord; The Lord shall enlighten my darkness." Or "To shine on those living in darkness and in the shadow of death, to guide our feet into the path of peace." (Luke 1:79).

It doesn't take much thinking to see the absurdity of this argument. As Christian Author and Apologist Dr. H.C. Felder stated:

"… This does not apply to humans since every person has light in them being made in the image of God regardless of the external color of their skin … This line of reasoning leads to absurd, illogical conclusions. Is a panther more evil than a lion? Is a raven eviler than a dove? ... Are light-skinned blacks less evil than darker-skinned blacks? ... Are Swedish people godlier than Italians since they tend to be of a lighter hue? ..." [36]

It is easy to see the foolishness in this type of reasoning.

---

[35] H. C. Felder, *The African American Guide to the Bible*, 208-210.
[36] Ibid. 214.

Racism in the Bible

As alluded to earlier, racism has been around almost as long as human beings and is shown in both the Old and New Testaments in the Bible. We can be certain that God only made one race, the human race and does not tolerate racism (Acts 10:34). We see how God dealt with racism early in the Bible with the story that centered around Moses and his siblings, Aaron and Miriam. Moses, who was Hebrew, married a Cushite (African woman) and was quickly criticized by his brother Aaron and sister Miriam for doing so (Num. 12:1-2). When God heard this, He was angry and immediately called Moses, Aaron, and Miriam to the tent where He scolded Miriam and Aaron. After a cloud was lifted from the tent, Miriam's skin was as white as snow, for God had stricken her with leprosy. When Aaron saw his sister in this unsightly condition, he obviously felt sorry for her because he pleaded with Moses to ask God to reverse this situation and Moses pleaded with God. God told Moses to put Miriam outside the camp for seven days, then bring her back, at which point she was apparently healed of leprosy (vs.10-15).

The Scripture shows that God was not merely displeased with Miriam, He was actually "Angry" with her (vs 9). It was obviously Miriam who voiced the criticism rather than Aaron since it was she on whom God brought the more serious discipline of leprosy. Leprosy causes skin sores, nerve, muscle weakness, and other physical problems, including being unpleasant to look upon. So in Miriam's situation her skin was "White as snow" which also meant embarrassment. It was as if God was telling her, "So you want a lighter-skinned sister-in-law? Well, since you like light-skin so much, I will make your skin lighter for a while." One thing that amazes me is how those who use the Bible to justify slavery and oppression never mentions this story.

We can also point to an example of racism in the New Testament and see how Jesus dealt with it. This story took place in the city of Samaria which was an ancient capital of the northern Kingdom of Israel and is told in the fourth chapter of the Gospel of John. To get from Judea to Galilee, the most direct route was to go through Samaria. However, the Jews didn't normally take that route because the Jews had a strong dislike for the Samaritan people. They saw the Samaritans as an inferior race of people and were prejudiced towards them. Why was this and who were the Samaritans?

In 722 BC God brought judgment on the Jewish people by having the Assyrians attack Israel. When the Assyrians attacked Israel, they brought some of the Jews back to Assyria and transplanted some Assyrians into Israel. This led to intermarriages and the children from these marriages were Samaritans – half-Jews and half-Assyrians. The Jews saw them as half-breeds and an inferior race of people. They saw them as lowlife, underclass, and sometimes referred to them as Samaritan dogs. The Jews stayed away from the Samaritans but when Jesus, who was a Jew, went to Galilee, He went straight through Samaria and when He reached a little town called Sychar, He sat down by a well.

One interesting point in this story is that when John wrote this, he specifically stated that the well was Jacob's well (John 4:6). This is significant because Jacob gave this well to his son Joseph, so this was not an ordinary well. This well had historic significance because it could be traced through Joseph all the way back to Jacob. And while the Jews didn't get along with the Samaritans and the Samaritans didn't get along with the Jews, they both loved Jacob. Jacob was looked upon as the father of the Jews, but he was also the father of the Samaritans because, even though the Samaritans were only part Jewish, they accepted the first five books of the Bible. Jacob is in the first book of the Bible, Genesis and the Samaritans accepted the first book of the Bible, therefore they accepted Jacob.

So Jacob was the common denominator between the Jews and the Samaritans – they both love Jacob. So Jesus, being a Jew, used a wise strategy to drive home His point. He met the Samaritan woman at the well on common ground – a place of agreement (Vs. 7-9). The Samaritan woman knew Jesus was a Jew even though He didn't tell her but how did she know He was a Jew? It was obviously evident because Jesus looked like a Jew, dressed like a Jew, and talked like a Jew. In other words, Jesus didn't try to hide who He was. He made it abundantly clear who He was by maintaining His racial and cultural identity when He confronted her. But even though He maintained His racial identity, He didn't let it get in the way of doing what His Father had called Him to do. He wanted her to know that He was a Jew.

In essence, Jesus was saying, I'm a Jew but I don't hate you because you're from a different race. I don't look down upon you because you are of a different race. Notice also in this story that Jesus sent the other Jewish disciples back to get food. However, when they got back with the food, Jesus told them that He wasn't hungry. He told them that He has food that they don't know anything about (vs 31-34). What happened? It was clear that Jesus did this to get them out of the way because of their racist attitude toward Samaritans. He knew that they would interfere with Him witnessing to this woman. He knew how they felt about the Samaritans. They couldn't witness the Samaritans because of their racist hatred toward them.

This is how racist attitudes among Christians can affect our witness for Jesus. Racism destroys our witness for Jesus Christ and we can't be effective in our efforts to glorify Him in the presence of others as we are told to do (1 Cor. 10:32). When we have prejudice or racism in our hearts toward those of a different race or economic status, not only do we cause division here and now, but our racist mindsets can have eternal consequences. We are to reach across racial and economic lines to get the gospel to others, whether they are black, white, Asian, Spanish, or any other color. We can be more effective when we see people as people, not as races. Notice how Jesus handled the racist situation. He sent His disciples back to get food; He met the Samaritan woman on neutral ground: He made sure she knew that He was a Jew; He asked her for water using her cup; Then He began witnessing to her. She ran home and told all the others, and many of the Samaritans were converted (John 4:28-29). Because Jesus was not prejudiced or racist, many people were brought to Christ, and many people gained eternal life.

God makes it abundantly clear that Christians should not display superior feelings towards others (Phil. 2:3). Paul told Timothy to keep his teachings and instructions without partiality and to do nothing out of favoritism (1 Tim. 5:21). And when he told the Colossians that, "Here there is neither Greek nor Jew, circumcised nor uncircumcised, barbarian, Scythian, slave nor free, but Christ is all and in all," he covered four different classes of ethnicities: (Gentile or Jew), religious distinctions, (Circumcised or uncircumcised), cultural distinctions (Barbarian or Scythian) economic distinctions, and slave or free (Col. 3:11). Clearly this is meant to include all human beings.

Slavery in the Bible

When we speak of slavery today, we usually and immediately have the image of black slaves on plantations in the antebellum south working hard, being beaten, raped, and lynched. When the Bible talks about slavery, it is talking about a completely different situation. Slavery in the Bible was more in tune with that of an indentured servant. An indentured servant was a person that worked under contract for another person for a definite period of time (e.g., 7 years) for free passage to a new country or for some other economic benefit. You may have remembered being taught in high school history classes that during the seventeenth century, most of the white laborers in Maryland and Virginia came from England as indentured servants. In early colonial America paying for passage to America was far too expensive for many people so they simply sold themselves out, working in households or apprenticeship positions until they paid back their debts to their "Boss" or "Employer."

Old Testament servanthood was very similar, and the words "Master" or "Slaves" are too strong words for this situation. A baseball player traded to another team with another "owner" now "belongs" to that team and owner. However, no one would call this slavery. This would be a formal contractual agreement which is similar to the Old Testament servant/employee arrangements. Servanthood in the Old Testament was more like colonial America than the antebellum South. There were many laws regulating what owners could and could not do. Consider the following:

If a slave was injured, for example, if an employer gouged out the eye of a slave accidentally or intentionally, that slave was to be set free (Exo. 21:26-27). Furthermore, if an employer's discipline resulted in the immediate death of the slave, that owner (master) was to be punished (Exo. 21:20).

If a servant were kidnapped, whether he's kept or sold, the kidnapper is to be put to death. (Exo. 21:16). In addition, if the kidnapper beats up the servant or treats him violently or sells him, the kidnapper should be put to death (Deut. 24:7).

The Confederacy claims to follow the Bible faithfully regarding slavery, but the Fugitive Slave Law proved differently. The Fugitive Slave Law was passed by the United States Congress on September 18, 1850, and required escaped slaves, upon capture, to be returned to their slave owners whether or not captured in a slave or free state. This was in stark contrast to the biblical law on runaway slaves. Israel was commanded to offer safe harbor to runaway slaves (Deut. 23:15-16).

In the New Testament, Paul and other writers were vehemently opposed to dehumanization and oppression of others, including slaves. The idea that slaves were mere property was out of the question and the status of slave or free was irrelevant (Gal. 3:28; Col. 3:11). In Ephesians 5 and Colossians 4 Paul gave household rules for both Christian slaves and Masters. And in Ephesians 6 he made it clear that Masters were to "… Treat your slaves in the same way. Do not threaten them, since you know that he who is both their Master and yours is in heaven, and there is no favoritism with him." (Ephes. 6:9, NIV)

Slavery in the Bible can be summarized as follows:

1. It was essentially intended as a means to relieve the poor of their crushing economic burdens. It was salvation from starvation for many.
2. It was for a limited period of just seven years, after which release was to be complete and final, unless the slave (servant) preferred to stay.
3. Debt-servants were to be treated with full human dignity.
4. Injured servants were to be released.

5. The practice of kidnapping persons to enslave them was outlawed.
6. Runaway slaves were to be given safe harbor.[37]

So when we consider the views of those who used the Bible to justify slavery during the antebellum South (or anytime afterward) it is clear that their views are diametrically opposite in most cases, and completely off base in others concerning the biblical laws.

Blacks Inferior to Whites?

Doesn't the Bible teach that blacks are inferior to whites? This is a belief that has been held by whites and blacks during the periods before and after slavery. In order to justify the institution of slavery and oppression of blacks, many whites turned to the Bible. Here Scriptures were taken out of context, improperly interpreted, and falsely applied to support the view of slaveholders and segregationists. After all, who could deny the institution of slavery and white supremacy when this view is set forth in the Bible by God Himself? This was reinforced by popular whites like Jefferson Davis (before becoming Confederate President) who said before Congress.

"The low and vulgar son of Noah, who laughed at his father's exposure, sunk by debasing himself and his lineage by a connection with an inferior race of men, he doomed his descendants to perpetual slavery."[38]

By relating the story of Noah to the institution of slavery, Jefferson validated slavery and supported his views that blacks were inferior to whites.

---

[37] Paul Copan, *Is God a Moral Monster*; 129-132.
[38] H. C. Felder, *The African American Guide to the Bible,* 231-232.

Senator Robert Byrd of West Virginia, while filibustering against the 1964 Civil Rights Act, read the Authorized Version of Genesis 9:18-27 and remarked, "Noah apparently saw fit to discriminate against Ham's descendants in that he placed a curse upon Canaan." He used this to defend his view that the Civil Rights Act was an anti-biblical law.[39]

This view that blacks are inferior to whites according to the Bible was so convincing and so common that even blacks believed and held onto it. In the 1930s, a former slave by the name of Gus "Jabbo" Rogers said the following in an interview:

"God gave [religion] to Adam and took it away from Adam and gave it to Noah, and you know, Miss, Noah had three sons, and when Noah got drunk on wine, one of his sons laughed at him, and the other two took a sheet and walked backward and threw it over Noah. Noah told the one who laughed, 'Your children will be hewers of wood and drawers of water for the other two children and they be known by their hair and their skin behind dark.' So, Miss, there we are, and that is the way God meant us to be. We have always had to follow the white folks and do what we saw them do, and that's all there is to it. You just can't get away from what the Lord said." [40]

The idea that the Bible supports the notion that blacks are inferior is absurd in every aspect. Dr. HC Felder noted the following in his well-researched book on, *The African American Guide to the Bible:*

"The inferiority of any race is not supported in the Bible. Those who advance this idea of racial inferiority is based on the

---

[39] Ibid. 234.
[40] Ibid. 233.

belief that God separated humanity by race. We have already argued against this position."

The idea of race is not one that even existed during the times covered by the Bible or in the Bible at all. God and the Bible dealt with people based on nations, not color or physical characteristics.

Blacks cannot possibly be inferior to whites since we are all African. This goes back to the scientific evidence mentioned earlier that human civilization began in Africa. All white people can trace their ancestry to blacks.

The Bible mentions blacks in a favorable light on numerous occasions. As evidence against the curse, the very first man to be a mighty one in the earth Nimrod, a descent from Ham, who built the great city Nineveh. The posterity of Abraham, who descended from Shem, was carried captive into Assyria, of which Nineveh was the capital. Therefore, the Jews were actually enslaved by descendants of Africans." [41]

Dr. Felder noted how blacks are presented in the Bible in positive ways under various situations:

1. The mighty men of Ethiopia and Put who handle the shield (Jer. 46:9).
2. The Old Testament indicates that black people were part of the Hebrew army (2 Sam. 18:21-32).
3. Two of the twelve tribes of Israel, Manasseh and Ephraim, were born to Joseph from an Egyptian woman (Gen. 46:20).
4. Moses married an Ethiopian woman (Num. 12:1).
5. The prevailing portrait of the Ethiopians in the Old Testament is that of wealthy people (Job 28:19; Isaiah 45:14).

---

[41] Ibid. 235.

6. "Zephaniah, son of Cush" (Zeph. 1) may indicate that one of the books of the Old Testament was authored by a black African.
7. Matthew, Mark, and Luke report an African helped Jesus carry his cross (Matt. 27:32); Mark 15:21); Luke 23:26; compare John 19:17).
8. God performed a miracle to bring salvation to the first Gentile convert who was an Ethiopian eunuch, a court official of Candace, queen of the Ethiopians (Acts 8:27).

Dr. Felder continued his narrative on this subject by stating that, "Although this list is not exhaustive, these examples should be sufficient to demonstrate that *the Bible does not consider black evil, cursed, or inferior.*" [42]

The Bible has never supported the idea that one race, ethnicity, or group of people are to be superior to another. In fact, the Bible states just the opposite (Deut. 10:17; Acts 17:26; Acts 10:34; Rom. 2:11; Ephes. 6:9). But what about the Jewish people? Didn't God choose them as better than other nations? Not at all, God chose the Jewish people as His special people, not because they were better or greater than other nations but because He made a covenant with their Father Abraham (Deut. 7:7-9). More specifically, as we read through the Scriptures, we will see that God chose the Jewish people to:

1. Give testimony to a Pure and Powerful, Almighty God.
2. Give testimony to blessings received when they were obedient.
3. Give them the oracles or Word of God (the Bible).
4. Bring forth the Messiah (Jesus Christ).

---

[42] Ibid. 236.

This we know because not only does the Bible gives Scriptural support for this, but a review of Jewish history shows this is what the Jewish people brought to the world.

Was Jesus White?

This is a question that comes up frequently among Christians as well as those in other religions. Many people want Jesus to look like people in their own race, ethnic group or culture, and portray Him in that way. Europeans frequently show Jesus with blond hair, blue eyes, and other physical features of a white European. Africans often paint or draw Jesus as dark with African features. Asians may show Jesus to look Asian. It is important to know that the Bible does not describe Jesus' physical appearance, but it does give us sufficient information to know how Jesus must have looked.

Speaking of Jesus in Isaiah, we read the following in Isaiah:

"He had no form or majesty that we should look at him, and no beauty that we should desire him." (Isa. 53:2, ESV).

Isaiah is showing us that Jesus did not stand out as anyone unique or especially different or handsome in His physical appearance. In other word Jesus looked as a normal, ordinary man among the people He grew up with and was around. According to the Bible, Jesus was a Jew (Matt. 1:2). He lived in the Middle East and was of Semitic descent, meaning that He certainly would not have had white skin, blue eyes, and blond hair. As a Middle-Eastener, Jesus would have had light to medium-brown skin and dark brown to black hair. Occasionally, we see some Middle Easterners with lighter skin close to that of Europeans, but this is rare indeed. And since Isaiah indicates that Jesus was a normal looking person, this rarity would not likely have applied to Him.

Whichever of these variants Jesus had, He was not the white man as depicted in many of the photos and paintings we see today.

Other reasons we know Jesus was not white are as follows:[43]

- Jesus is a descendant of Abraham (Matt. 1:1). Abraham was from Ur of the Chaldeans, an area populated by Nimrod, son of Cush. Cush was the founder of the African nations (Sudan, Ethiopia, and parts of Egypt today).
- Jesus came from the line of Judah (Matt. 1:2). Judah married Canaanite women (Gen. 38:7; 1 Chron. 2:3, 4). The Canaanites were descents of Canaan who was the son of Ham, the Father of the African nations.
- Jesus was a descendant of Rahab, a Canaanite prostitute who helped save the Hebrew spies who were scouting the promised Land, which would become Israel (Josiah 2).
- Before she married King David, Bathsheba was married to Uriah the Hittite and was most likely a Hittite herself, a descendent of Ham.

Was Jesus black?

Many blacks assert that Jesus is black and usually show Him as black in pictures, paintings, and drawings, but was Jesus black? In 1924, the General Assembly of Virginia passed into law the Racial Integrity Act of 1924 to prevent whites and blacks from marrying. This Act describes white persons in the following manner:

"… For the purpose of this act, the term "White person" shall apply only to the person who has no trace whatsoever of any blood other than Caucasian but persons who have one-sixteenth or less of the blood of the American Indian and have no other non-Caucasic

---

[43] Ibid. 180.

blood shall be deemed to be white persons. All laws heretofore passed and now in effect regarding the intermarriage of white and colored persons shall apply to marriages prohibited by this act."[44]

This means that any person having *one drop* of black blood is considered black, or if you were deemed to have any non-white blood, you were considered black. This being the case, Jesus would certainly be considered black based on His lineage as described above. It is important to remember however, that Jesus' race, culture, or ethnicity has nothing at all to do with Him being the Savior of the world. People generally and naturally want Jesus to be like them, but our job is to be like Jesus (Phil. 2:5) and get away from this racist ideology that the enemy has used to divide people and cause death all over the world from the beginning of mankind. As children of God and followers of Jesus Christ, we must not let ourselves fall prey to these types of sinful views.

---

[44] *An Act to Preserve Racial Integrity;*
http://www2.vcdh.virginia.edu/lewisandclark/students/projects/monacans/Conte mporary_Monacans/racial.html

CHAPTER 5
IS THE UNITED STATES SYSTEMICALLY RACIST?

"And you shall know the truth, and the truth shall make you free."
(John 8:32)

What is Systemic Racism?

The term "Systemic Racism" was coined by sociologist Dr. Joe Feagin. In the introduction of his book, "Racist America: Roots, Current Realities, and Future Reparations," Dr. Feagin defined systemic racism as follows:

"Systemic racism includes the complex array of antiblack practices, the unjustly gained political-economic power of whites, the continuing economic and other resource inequalities along racial lines, and the white racist ideologies and attitudes created to maintain and rationalize white privilege and power. Systemic here means that the core racist realities are manifested in each of society's major parts [...] each major part of U.S. society—the economy, politics, education, religion, the family—reflects the fundamental reality of systemic racism." [45]

In other words, systemic racism generally means that race-based discrimination is seen as ingrained and woven into the laws,

---

[45] Joe Feagan, *Racist America: Roots, Current Realities, and Future Reparations,* 6.

policies, and traditions, that affect virtually every aspect of our lives, including the family. This essentially means that racism can emerge in any situation, even if the people involved aren't racist. If the United States fits into this category, it is systematically racist in a way that for all practical purposes, does not change. In fact, it cannot change without being uprooted from its foundation and another foundation is put in its place. This is precisely what many are trying to do in the United States today, restructure the United States into a different type of government by first destroying it, then initiating a socialist or communist system of government other than the Constitutional Republic we now attempt to operate under. But the question, for now, is: Is the United States systematically racist to begin with? Or can we demonstrate that the United States began as a systemically racist nation?

Based on the definition provided by Dr. Feagan, this can be easily determined. Since systemic racism implies being woven into the foundation of a nation, we should look at the founding documents of the United States to determine how and why it was established and move on up through the history of the nation to the period in which we now live. This will show us if the United States is or is not systemically racist. First, it would help to keep in mind that it is God who establishes nation (Acts 17:26) and God had specific purposes for establishing all nations, including the United States. The reasons and purposes God established on certain nations is beyond the scope of this book, but it is sufficient for now to know that it is God, not man, who established every nation. For what is now the United States, the backdrop began in England when King James was actually persecuting Christians because he did not like their reformation teachings. Christians in England were not allowed religious freedom, so many of them got together and asked the King if they could move over to this new world (now the

United States). King James granted them their request and on September 6, 1620, 102 passengers, including 50 men, 19 women and 33 young adults gathered on a ship called the Mayflower and set sail for America. This was a difficult trip that lasted for two months, and they fought the harsh elements of a storm-tossed sea, but they eventually landed in what is now Plymouth, Massachusetts, commonly referred to today as having landed on Plymouth Rock.

It is important to notice that the men God chose to establish the United States were God-fearing men as they were in search of a geographical location where they could freely practice their religion. Also, even before these men got off the ship, they drafted a document called the Mayflower Compact which was signed by 41 of the 50 men on board.[46] They wanted to worship freely, they wanted fair government for all without the rulership of a king, and they wanted to advance the purpose of God. Notice how they began the Compact:

"IN THE NAME OF GOD, AMEN. We, whose names are underwritten, the Loyal Subjects of our dread Sovereign Lord King James, by the Grace of God, of Great Britain, France, and Ireland, King, Defender of the Faith, &c. Having undertaken for the Glory of God, and Advancement of the Christian Faith, and the Honour of our King and Country, a Voyage to plant the first Colony in the northern Parts of Virginia …"

This excerpt from the Mayflower Compact alone gives us the intent of the forefathers in establishing America. It was for the "Glory of God, and Advancement of the Christian Faith." This

---

[46] *https://www.history.com/search?q=mayflower%20compact*

gives us some idea of what these men had in mind when establishing a new nation.

Declaration of Independence

Then as we fast forward to the period before the Revolutionary War was over, God had these early Americans, now organized as 13 colonies, established a Continental Congress and drafted a statement which announced their independence from Great Britain. This document was called the Declaration of Independence and the 13 original Colonies were now an independent nation, free from England. So, let's look at a few of the words of the Declaration of Independence.

"We hold these truths to be self-evident, that all men are created equal, that they are endowed by their Creator with certain unalienable Rights, that among these are Life, Liberty and the pursuit of Happiness.--That to secure these rights, Governments are instituted among Men, deriving their just powers from the consent of the governed, --That whenever any Form of Government becomes destructive of these ends, it is the Right of the People to alter or to abolish it, and to institute new Government …"

This Declaration is frequently referred to as the Birth Certificate of the United States, signed July 1, 1776, and officially adopted on July 4, 1776, the day we celebrate today as Independence Day.[47] Thomas Jefferson drafted this document but it was signed by 55 others; 50 were known Christian and 29 had seminary or Bible College degrees. Notice what it says: First, it says these truths are self-evident that we are all created equal. This

---

[47] *https://www.history.com/news/9-things-you-may-not-know-about-the-declaration-of-independence*

is based on the Apostle Paul's letter to the Galatians which stated, "There is neither Jew nor Greek, there is neither slave nor free, there is neither male nor female; for you are all one in Christ Jesus." (Gal. 3:28).

Many people today claim when the Declaration states that "All men are created equal" the Founding Fathers really meant to say "All white men are created equal." However, this is definitely not the case as Jefferson himself explicitly identified slaves as men when addressing another issue of his draft, meaning that slaves are included in the American promise.[48] When the Declaration of Independence goes on to say that we are endowed by our Creator with certain unalienable rights – its acknowledging that we have a Creator (In the beginning God ... Gen. 1:1). It says among these rights are life, liberty, and the pursuit of happiness. Jefferson is saying that our rights come from God, not the government. There is more written in this Declaration, but these are the principles that were written for the nation to live by. It must be considered that since most of the signers of this document were known Christians, they must have had some belief and intentions in doing what is morally right.

The U.S. Constitution

But there was another main document that God led these Founding Fathers to adopt, and that document is called the Constitution. It was in the summer of 1787, September 17th that the U.S. Constitution was signed by 39 Founding Fathers, again, most of whom were Christians. So these early Americans declared their independence from England and they had been operating under the Articles of Confederation but now they adopted a U.S. Constitution (went into effect on March 4, 1789). But God also had

---

[48] Wallbuilders, *America's Exceptional History of Anti-Slavery;* April 6, 2020.

to make sure that this Constitution, that would be the legal foundation on which the nation was to operate by, would reflect biblical principles, i.e., based on the Bible, or He would not be able to bless the nation with riches and protection (Psalm 33:12). The men that drafted the Constitution were godly men and these men saw fit to establish the Constitution on biblical principles. They knew that men were basically selfish, so they didn't want to give all power to one branch of government. So they separated the government into three branches (Legislative, Judicial, and Executive branches). They received this idea of three branches of government from reading Isaiah 33:22, which states as follows:

For the Lord is our judge, [Judicial Branch], the Lord is our lawgiver, [Legislative Branch], the Lord is our king; [Executive Branch], it is he who will save us.

Not only that, but the Founders view the character of men from a biblical perspective so they knew that man left to himself would engage in selfish activities rather than doing the will of the American people. Jeremiah 17:9 says, "The heart is deceitful above all things, And desperately wicked; Who can know it?" When explaining the necessity of separation of powers, Founder John Adams cited Jeremiah 17:9 on multiple occasions. Other Founding Fathers (e.g., George Washington, Alexander Hamilton, and James Madison) were in full agreement.

Federalist 51 stated the following:

"What is government itself but the greatest of all reflections on human nature? If men were angels, no government would be necessary. In framing a government which is to be administered by men over men, the great difficulty lies in this: you must first enable the government to control the governed, and in the next place oblige it to control itself."

Even the type of tax-exempt status given to churches was taken from the Bible. Notice below:

Also we inform you that it shall not be lawful to impose tax, tribute, or custom on any of the priests, Levites, singers, gatekeepers, Nethinim, or servants of this house of God (Ezra 7:24).

This tax-exempt status is still being used by churches and other non-profits institutions today under Internal Revenue Code Section 501.

A few other examples to verify that the U.S. Constitution is based on the Bible are as follows:

Article 1 Section 8 for immigration laws came from Leviticus 19:34. "The stranger who dwells among you shall be to you as one born among you, and you shall love him as yourself; for you were strangers in the land of Egypt: I am the LORD your God."

Article 2, Section 1 of the Constitution says a president must be a citizen of the US. This came from Deuteronomy where God told Israel, "… you shall surely set a king over you whom the Lord your God chooses; *one* from among your brethren you shall set as king over you; you may not set a foreigner over you, who *is* not your brother." (Deut. 17:15).

Article 3, Section 3 of the Constitution says there must be 2 witnesses for treason (which is punishable by death). "Whoever is deserving of death shall be put to death on the testimony of two or three witnesses; he shall not be put to death on the testimony of one witness (Deut. 17:6).

Some have stated that the Constitution is racist and point to the Three-Fifth Clause as support for their assertion. The Three-Fifth Clause of the Constitution reads as follows:

"Representatives and direct Taxes shall be apportioned among the several States which may be included within this Union, according to their respective Numbers, which shall be determined by adding to the whole Number of free Persons, including those bound to Service for a Term of Years, and excluding Indians not taxed, three-fifths of all other Persons." (Art. I, § 2, cl. 3).

Some believe that this clause shows blacks as only "three-fifths" of a person, rather than a whole individual and is therefore racist. However, an understanding of the legislative history shows that this clause was included in the Constitution to help put an end to slavery, thereby treating blacks as regular citizens. The Constitution had established that every State would get one Representative for every 30,000 inhabitants of that State. The southern slave states saw this as a great opportunity to get many Representatives in Congress and expand the slave trade if they could count all of their slaves as inhabitants. This would have been a windfall for slaveholders because there were hundreds of thousands of slaves in Southern States at the time. However, anti-slavery Founders in the North were vehemently opposed to this and the debate was on as to include or not include slaves when determining how many Representatives a state may have. The final compromise was that the Southern States could count each slave as three-fifths as a person for Representative purposes rather than one whole person. This way, the South could not have too many Representatives to vote and keep the slave trade going. Therefore, the Three-Fifth Clause, which dealt with representatives in Congress and had absolutely nothing to do with the worth of a slave or any other individual, was added to the Constitution; it was added to help blacks by attempting to put an end to the institution of slavery.

These are just some examples showing how the Constitution is mostly based on biblical principles but continue reading as we provide more information to substantiate this point.

The Constitution was written and signed by mainly God-fearing men but there are people today who do not like this country or the Constitution, so they continuously try to convince others that the country was not founded based on biblical principles. Many other nations recognize the uniqueness of the U.S. Constitution and founding documents and have expressed their amazement at how the United States has not had to change its Constitution. There has never been any nation on earth that has had a Constitution as God gave the United States.

According to the World Atlas, there are 195 countries in the world (193 members of the United Nations plus two non-member observer states the Vatican and Palestine).[49] These countries are scattered over 7 continents today, and includes a worldwide population of close to 8 million people. Political Scientists and historians have tried to figure out what made the U.S. Constitution so different than the Constitutions of all other nations (i.e., those nations that have Constitutions because many nations operate without a formal, official Constitution). So they studied, reviewed, and analyzed approximately 15,000 documents used in establishing the U.S. Constitution to see where the Founding Fathers got the knowledge and information. Guess what they found? They found 3,154 quotations coming directly from the Bible![50] This is amazing!

---

[49] Ellen Kershner, World Geography, *How Many Countries are in the World?* August 26, 2020.
[50] Donald S. Lutz, *"The Relative Influence of European Writers on Late Eighteenth Century American Political Thought,"* American Political Science Review, Vol. 78, Issue 1, March 1984, 191.

Any honest person knowing this information would have to conclude that the US Constitution was based on the Holy Bible. Furthermore, the US Constitution is the longest ongoing Constitution in the history of the world. We have never had to change our Constitution, even though there has been and will continue to be Amendments. No other nation even came close to this record. In fact, many nations have changed their entire Constitutions numerous times.

To be systemic racist, the United States would have to have racist policies and laws in place, but as we've seen, the two main founding documents, the Declaration of Independence and the U.S. Constitution was biblically based and did not include racist policies or overtones. Some say yes, that may be true, but the U.S. Constitution was written for whites only. First of all, there is no evidence for that, but it is easily understood why many blacks feel this way.

The primary reason is that the laws of the Constitution have not always been applied equally to all races in the United States. However, this does not make the Constitution itself a racist document, instead it is the distortion and misuse of the Constitution by racist men that is the problem. It's how the Constitution was misused that presents the problem. It's like saying the Internet is bad because it contains propaganda, terrorist recruiting, and pornography, when we know the Internet provides tremendous benefits to billions of people and businesses worldwide. Nevertheless, there have been a variety of local policies and laws put in place through several States in America that blatantly denied the Constitutional rights of blacks. These laws, primarily in the southern part of the country where slavery was most active, were referred to as "Jim Crow" laws and were racist and oppressive to blacks (and other minorities). Again, this does not make the Constitution racist, it would make the State and local laws racist, though some may say that the United States is systemically racist at least in part, since some of the States enacted racist laws.

So let's just say for the sake of argument that Jim Crow laws were enacted in some states and the U.S. Constitution was written for and applied only to whites. If this were the case, we could say that the U.S. is systemically racist at least for the time when these laws were in place. But is this really the case today? A brief review of U.S. history does not bear this out as those laws have been abolished and/or amended and no longer apply. This means that we cannot honestly say the country is systemically racist. Consider the following:

- The Civil War was fought to decide the issue of slavery once and for all and during the war, in 1863, President Abraham Lincoln issued the Emancipation Proclamation, freeing slaves in the states that were in rebellion against the union. There were approximately 800,000 casualties in the bloodiest war ever fought in the nation, simply to put an end to slavery.
- In 1864 the 14th Amendment was ratified. This Amendment guaranteed that former slaves and all Americans would receive due process and equal protection under the law from their state governments.
- In 1870 the 15th Amendment was adopted. This Amendment guaranteed the right to vote for African-Americans and was championed by President Ulysses S. Grant.
- In 1875, the Civil Rights Act was passed. This Act barred discrimination in public accommodations and on public conveyances on land and water and prohibited exclusion of African Americans from jury duty.

- In 1871 the Third Force Act was passed. This Act, also known as the KKK Act, was used by President Grant to deploy federal troops to defeat the Ku Klux Klan.
- In 1875, the Civil Rights Act was passed. This Act barred discrimination in public accommodations and on public conveyances on land and water and prohibited exclusion of African Americans from jury duty.
- In 1957 the Civil Rights Act created the Civil Rights Commission and the Civil Rights Division in the Justice Department. This was supported by President Dwight D. Eisenhower.
- In 1954 the U.S. Supreme Court rendered a decision in Brown v. Board of Education which ended legal segregation in schools. President Eisenhower sent in the 101st Airborne Division to Little Rock, Arkansas, to protect black students being integrated into Central High School.
- In 1962 President John F. Kennedy federalized the Mississippi National Guard and the Alabama National Guard to maintain order during the integration of the University of Mississippi and in 1963, the University of Alabama.
- In 1964 the Civil Rights Act was passed. This Act, passed under President Lyndon B. Johnson ended segregation in public places and banned employment discrimination on the basis of race, color, religion, sex or national origin.
- In 1965 the Voting Rights Act was passed. This Act, passed under President Lyndon B. Johnson, was aimed at overcoming legal barriers at the state and local levels that prevented African Americans from exercising their right to vote as guaranteed under the 15th Amendment to the U.S.

These are some of the main laws passed in the United States to prevent racism and discrimination in its systems and laws.

Systemic racism implies ongoing racism embedded in the system or foundation of the country. If the United States were systemically racist, the Civil War would not have been fought and none of these laws would have passed. This is not to say that there is not racism in the country, this is to say that racism is not woven into the foundational laws and policies in the country as Dr. Feagin's definition implies, and therefore we cannot honestly say the country is systemically racist. Stated differently, racism is not legally incorporated in the system of Federal, State, and Local laws today.

Why then do we have so much racism and oppression of blacks and other minorities in the country? First, there is not as much racism and oppression in the country as many in the news media would have us to believe, especially not the traditional racism that we've experienced in the past. Second, the racism that we have in this country is for the same reason it has always been in all nations since the beginning of mankind. The human heart is evil and wicked (Jer. 17:9) and we as human beings have an inherent selfishness about ourselves (2 Tim. 3:1-2) with a strong love for money (1 Tim. 6:10). But the racism we see today is practiced by relatively small groups of selfish individuals and not racism for the nation as a whole, or even large segments of the nation. The enemy uses these individual acts of racism and projects them onto the nation as a whole, the news media runs with this false narrative, the public schools, colleges, and universities indoctrinate students with this misleading, inaccurate, deceptive teaching, and this causes division among the entire nation, which is what we're seeing today.

Racial Criminal Justice System

Politicians, other prominent figures, the news media, and even the church continuously assert that the United States has a racist criminal justice system. When you look at the news media and listen to what's being expounded daily, this certainly seems to be the case. At a Presidential Debate on Martin Luther King Day in 2008, President Obama stated that blacks and whites "Are arrested at very different rates, are convicted at very different rates, [and] receive very different sentences ... for the same crime."

Presidential Candidate Hillary Clinton stated how it is a "Disgrace of a criminal-justice system that incarcerates so many more African-Americans proportionately than whites." Obviously, a person hearing these statements and watching the evening news would not disagree with these assertions. But amazingly enough, when we carefully review and analyze the statistics, the truth (which is what Christians should always look for) that emerges shows something differently. People holding this view see a biased legal system and harsh, severe drug enforcement as the two main reasons for a racist criminal justice system. So let's look at the facts surrounding them both.

According to the Federal Bureau of Justice Statistics, from 1976 to 2005, blacks committed over 52 percent of all murders in the United States. In 2006 the rate for blacks arrested for most crimes was two to nearly three times blacks' representation in the population. Furthermore, blacks constituted 39.3 percent of all violent-crime arrests, including 56.3 percent of all robbery and 34.5 percent of all aggravated-assault arrests and 29.4 percent of all property-crime arrests. The arrests statistics were similar for 2013.[51]

Reviewing these statistics show that blacks are responsible for the majority of crimes even though they make up only 13% of the population. Since this is the case, doesn't it follow that blacks would be arrested and incarcerated more than other groups? But, one may ask, couldn't this also show that blacks are arrested more frequently than whites even though the crime may be equal or less severe? Not at all, as further investigation shows the statistics on the race of criminals as reported by crime victims match the arrest data. In fact, going back as far as 1978, a study of robbery and aggravated assault in eight cities found consistency between the race of assailants in victim reports and arrests. This has been found to be true in a range of crimes across the board.[52]

Consider a more current set of statistics from the Federal Bureau of Investigation (FBI) National Crime Stats for 2019. The estimated number of murders in the nation was 16,425. Out of this total, known offenders were 11,493 and out of that total 6,425 were known, black offenders. This means that while blacks made up only 13.4% of the U.S. population, again, they were responsible for well over 50% of known murder offenders in 2019. If blacks are committing most of the crimes, shouldn't blacks be arrested more? Remember we're looking at this from a biblical perspective, that is with truth, honesty, and integrity.

Still, there is a wide assertion that police are biased against blacks which leads to a more frequent illegitimate arrest. Research on this topic has proven this theory to be false. In 2016, Roland Fryer, a black Harvard Professor, published the results of a

---

[51] Heather MacDonald, *The War on Cops*, 152.
[52] Ibid.

detailed, comprehensive study he and his teams completed. Professor Fryer stated that he started his study because of his anger over the deaths of Michael Brown and Freddie Gray. However, he admitted that his conclusions resulted in "the most surprising result of my career." This had been exhaustive research where Professor Fryer and his teams spent an estimated 3,000 hours reviewing the data from Los Angeles, Ca., three cities in Texas (Houston, Austin, and Dallas), and four counties and two cities in Florida (Orlando and Jacksonville). They examined 1,332 police shootings, fatal and non-fatal, in the police departments of 10 large cities and he stated in his introduction that his study was conducted to understand, "The extent to which there are racial differences in police use of force and (if any) whether those differences might be due to discrimination by police or explained by other factors at the time of the incident …"[53]

The study found that cops were more likely to cuff, push to the ground, pepper spray or otherwise put their hands on a black suspect vs a white suspect, and there are racial differences on non-lethal uses of force. Blacks were found to endure 21.3 percent of some use of force in these types of crimes. However, when it came to lethal type crimes, Professor Fryer concluded:

"Yet, on the most extreme use of force – officer-involved shootings – we are unable to detect any racial differences in either the raw data or when accounting for controls."[54]

---

[53] Roland Fryer Jr., *An Empirical Analysis of Racial Differences in Police Use of Force*, 2.
[54] Ibid, 35.

The *Dailywire,* in a 2016 article, listed the following six conclusions from the study:[55]

1. Police are not more likely to fire on blacks than whites. In fact, blacks are 20% less likely to be fired on.
2. Blacks and whites involved in police shootings were equally likely to be carrying a weapon.
3. Blacks are more likely to be treated worse by officers when it comes to physical contact.
4. The notion that police officers' accounts are biased and unreliable is largely a myth.
5. Use of mobile video to document alleged police brutality is not impacting policing practices.
6. Fryer's study aligns with other research.

It is understandable why Professor Fryer was surprised at his findings, as the majority of people who read his study probably are. The news media has pushed the narrative so far in the opposite direction from Fryer's conclusion that many people would bet lots of money that there is racial discrimination by police in these cases. This is especially true when a white officer shoots a black suspect. When a black officer shoots a black suspect, it does not generate the same level of outrage as when a white officer shoots a black suspect, especially when the black suspect is unarmed. Interestingly enough, the findings in this study confirm similar findings in "The Reverse Racism Effect," a study by researchers at Washington State University. Something else that should be considered in this account is that most blacks shot in these altercations were defying police orders, assaulting the police, fleeing the police, or otherwise resisting arrest. Complying with

---

[55] John Bickley, *6 Facts From New Study Finding NO RACIAL BIAS Against Blacks In Police Shootings*, Dailywire.com; July 11, 2016.

the orders of the police officers, even if that officer is not following proper procedures or being rude otherwise, would eliminate practically all these tragedies. From a biblical perspective, it is important to know that police and law enforcement officers are put here by God for our protection; and we are told in the Scriptures to obey the orders of these officers (Rom. 13:1-5). If there are wrongdoings engaged in by the arresting officer, they can be addressed later in a court of law, not in the heat of the moment. When they are addressed in the heat of the moment, we see just what we have today; frequent claims of racism, chaos, and confusion.

White Privilege

The term white privilege has sprung up in recent years and is being used in ways to promote chaos and further the racial divide. The term was made famous in 1988 by Peggy McIntosh, a feminist and antiracist scholar who wrote an article entitled "White Privilege: Unpacking the Invisible Knapsack." This article listed several examples asserting that white people have many more privileges than those available to people of color. Dr. Nicki Lisa Cole, commented on McIntosh's work in her article, "Understanding and Defining White Privilege" as follows:

At the heart of the concept is the assertion that, in a racist society, white skin allows for an array of unearned privileges unavailable to people of color. Accustomed to their social status and the benefits that accompany it, White people tend not to acknowledge their White privilege. Learning about the experiences of people of color, however, may prompt Whites to admit to the advantages they have in society.

McIntosh's list of 50 privileges includes being regularly surrounded—in everyday life and in media representations—by people who look like you and having the ability to avoid those who do not. These privileges also include not being interpersonally or institutionally discriminated against on the basis of race; never feeling afraid to defend oneself or speak out against injustice for fear of retaliation; and, being viewed as normal and belonging, among others. The key point in McIntosh's list of privileges is that Americans of color do not typically enjoy or have access to them. In other words, they experience racial oppression—and White people benefit from this.[56]

Today, the term "White Privilege" has been expanded to show whites have privilege over all people of color in virtually every area of civilization, including labor, entertainment, education, politics, business, social events, sports, and even discussion on climate change. It is important however, to look at this claim from a biblical perspective, which means among other things we are looking for objective truth in all the dynamics involved in this issue.

The problem with the white privilege assertion is that when we look at the facts and the truth of the matter, we will find that white privilege is simply not true today. There was a time when this assertion was partially true and there are currently some periodic incidences where whites are privileged over people of color, but this is not the general experience found in today's society in the United States. Let's look at some facts. According to the Bureau of Labor Statistics for 2018, consider the following lines of evidence that argue against the white privilege assertion:

---

[56] *https://www.thoughtco.com/white-privilege-definition-3026087.*

Earnings. The median weekly earnings of full-time wage and salary workers in 2018 were $1,241 for Asian men, $1,002 for white men and $735 for black men.

Occupations. Fifty-four percent of employed Asians worked in management, professional, and related occupations, which is the highest paying major occupational category; compared with 41 percent of employed Whites, 31 percent of employed Blacks.

Employment. The employment-population ratio (the proportion of the population that is employed) was 61.6 percent for Asians, 60.7 percent for Whites, 58.3 percent for Blacks,

When we look at these statistics, we will see that Asians did better than whites in each category. Should we, therefore, conclude that there is Asian privilege? The Asian households make more money than anyone else, they have greater employment than anyone else and they have better, higher-paying jobs than anyone else. The question is why? The answer is found in stable families and education. Among people 25 years and older, Asians were the most likely of the groups (including Hispanics and other minorities) to have graduated from college: 63 percent of Asians in the labor force had a bachelor's degree and higher, compared with 41 percent of Whites, and 31 percent of Blacks.

When it comes to families, according to the U.S. Census Bureau, for 2018 the percentage of black children under the age of 18 living in single-parent households more than doubled that of whites and more than quadrupled that of Asians. While 65% of blacks lived in single-family households, there were 24% of whites and only 15% of Asians kids in the same category. Clearly there is a connection between the breakdown of the family unit and the level of achievement, as many studies have shown. This has nothing to do with white privilege.

White privilege would essentially mean that whites would be at the top in all of these categories but as we've seen, this is not the case. We all have privileges, but we benefit from them according to how much work and effort we put into utilizing these privileges; and how much training and education we get to develop knowledge and skills to help expand these privileges. People have privileges based on family, education, natural talent, opportunities, geographical location, and other factors. All these factors must be considered when we say who is privileged and who is not. But for the sake of argument, assume that white privilege is a fact to the exclusion of all other privileges.

Let's say that whites have it better simply by being born white. How on earth is that going to hold me back from what I aspire to accomplish? Booker T. Washington said, "I have begun everything with the idea that I could succeed, and I never had much patience with the multitudes of people who are always ready to explain why one cannot succeed." Booker T was right on target; too many blacks are always ready to explain why they can't succeed. Their explanation almost always is "racism." My promotions in life, on the job or anywhere else come from God, not man (Psalm 75:6-7). If I study diligently, work hard, and apply myself, I am going to make the necessary academic achievements to be successful at reaching my goals regardless of any privilege someone else has. In these academic achievements, I would have prepared myself for successful career positions and will succeed just as anyone else. This is a biblical principle that all Christians must keep in mind (Gal. 6:7; Prov. 22:29). This has been shown to be true continuously among all mankind, including millions of successful blacks.

Consider someone like Dr. Ben Carson for example. Dr. Ben Carson, a black man, grew up in a single-parent household after his parents separated when he was only 8 years old. However, with encouragement and inspiration from his mother and hard work, he became a world renowned neurosurgeon and later Secretary of Housing and Urban Development with the Trump Administration from 2017 to 2021. How did white privilege hold him back?

Consider Dr. Carole Swain. Carole Swain, a black woman, was one of twelve children who grew up in poverty, living in a shack, sharing two beds with her eleven siblings. She missed school whenever it snowed or was too cold because she didn't have shoes to wear. She dropped out of high school in the ninth grade and ended up living with her grandmother in Roanoke, VA. She earned a GED, worked as a cashier at McDonald's, a door-to-door salesperson, and an assistant in a retirement facility. She later earned an associate degree, magna cum laude B.A. in Criminal justice, a master's degree in political science and PH.D. in political science. She is now a retired professor of political science and law at Vanderbilt University, a frequent television analyst, and author of several books. Did white privilege hold her back?

Drs. Ben Carson and Carole Swain are just two blacks, male and female that are mentioned as an example, but this does not mean that one has to reach the status of Carson and Swain to be successful in life without blaming white privilege. There are millions of blacks who have worked hard, got educated, and lived productive, rewarding lives. Indeed, five of the ten richest black communities in America are in the state of Maryland. These are blacks who are doctors, lawyers, accountants, self-employed entrepreneurs, and other business owners who have worked hard, gotten educated, and acquired the assets they have today. Consider this fact: By 1905, Tuskegee University, a black university had produced more self-made millionaires than Harvard, Yale, and Princeton combined! This is an astounding statistic that was reported in the February 23, 2017 edition of *Forbes Magazine.*[57] How did white privilege hold them back? If White Privilege were such a significant impediment in our society, how did this happen? Then there are those blacks who have natural talent in sports, entertainment, arts, etc. Should these people be denigrated and besmirched because they have certain "privileges" that others do not? What we call white privilege today is simply an excuse used by many blacks and liberals to justify low achievement in life. It is another attack by the enemy to cause anger, chaos, and division among people, and as Christians, we must not allow ourselves to fall into this trap of blaming others and calling others racist. We see examples of this every day in the United States even to the extent where we have some white people apologizing for being white. How sad.

Racism and Politics

One may ask if the United States is not systematically racist, why is racism brought up in every political issue and discussion in the news media and seemingly everywhere else? The answer is since our nation has a history of racism, oppression of blacks and minorities, and abusive slavery, it is very easy for people to use this issue to accomplish their selfish desires, politically and otherwise. In the political arena, racism is especially helpful by dividing the voters into two main categories, oppressors and oppressed. There are lots of avenues one can take with this but the one most commonly used is to remind the black race (oppressed) that they were held down in the past and still held down today by the white race (oppressors) so they must vote for the particular party that will not oppress them but will do all things for their benefit. This of course, in reality, is just the opposite of what has

---

[57] Vince Everett Ellison, *The Iron Triangle*, 124.

really happened because, as we've said from the beginning, this is a spiritual problem, meaning, among other things, the enemy and his cohorts are behind the entire situation.

A brief review of true U.S. history will demonstrate what we're saying here but first, it is important to keep in mind that we are to look at this from a biblical perspective. This means that we are to look for truth, justice, honesty, integrity, and civility regardless of what political party we're talking about and what the conclusions are. In other words, even though we will use the names of major political parties for identification and illustration purposes, when we're looking at this from a biblical perspective, we look for truth regardless of which party is involved.

The darkest period of American history is considered by many to be the slavery era. When we look at this period in history, we see racism and abuse of blacks in a variety of ways and at the highest levels. The institution of slavery was legalized in the United States and abuse was condoned and supported by those in law enforcement and the justice system. This abuse included, beatings, rapes, lynching, kidnappings, break-up of families, forced illiteracy, and other forms of hurt perpetrated by whites against blacks. The political party that legalized and supported this institution was the Democratic Party.[58]

Some compassionate whites did not like this ongoing abuse and eventually formed another political party to put an end to slavery. This party was called the Republican Party[59] After President Lincoln signed the Emancipation Proclamation and freed the slaves, the Democratic Party formed a terrorist organization called

---

[58] David Barton, *American History in Black and White,* 18.
[59] Ibid., 21.

the Ku Klux Klan.[60] This evil, terrorist organization continued its abuse and torture of blacks and embraced the ongoing support of the Democratic Party. As various Civil Rights bills were introduced to give blacks their fair rights in the country according to the Constitution, the Democratic Party voted to block every one of these bills. In spite of all their attempts to prevent these bills from passing into law and keep segregation going, these bills were passed into law. The Democratic Party wanted to keep slavery going, segregation going and blacks ignorant. Today this is the same party that claims to have the best interest of blacks at heart, while still keeping blacks in slavery, a new kind of slavery. For example, during the slavery era, blacks worked to benefit white Democrat slave owners (very few Republicans owned slaves in 1860), endured systemic breakdown of the family unit, and incurred forced illiteracy.

Today white, and even some black Democrats use blacks to work for votes, single family households are the highest they've ever been since the Emancipation, and the illiteracy rate among blacks are astronomical. Today, the results are the same for blacks as they were during the slavery era, and the only change is the means to which those results are achieved as Inner-city blacks are still on the plantation (trapped in crime infested inner cities) and still working (voting) for the very people who's keeping them there. This shows how race is used for political gain, even among black politicians today. This also shows that the racism issue is a spiritual one, not simply one of black and white or whites against blacks.

When we say that the United States is systematically racist, to be honest, we must consider all of the aforementioned factors. Furthermore, in general, the white population in the United States

---

[60] Ibid., 49-50.

does not want to be labeled as racist and has bent over backwards, so to speak, to demonstrate that they aren't racist. An example of this is when they voted twice to place a black president in the White House. In addition, they have voted for black governors, black mayors, and hundreds of blacks have been placed in prominent governmental positions. In addition to this, if the United States is systematically racist, why is it that millions attempt to migrate from other countries, some even risking and giving up their lives to get here? As I write, there are more than 15,000 Haitians (blacks) living under a bridge in Del Rio, Texas. Some of these beautiful people have traveled approximately 2,000 miles in the hopes of getting into and living in the United States. They traveled through lakes and rivers, woods, jungles, mountainous and other rugged terrain to make this arduous journey. These travelers included males, females, children, adults, families, and pregnant women – all in an effort to get to the United States. Many of them have to endure rape, child molestation, sex trafficking, and other atrocities, and they are aware of these dangers before they begin their journey. Still, they put forth every effort to get to the United States. But why would they go through this to live in a country if that country is so blatantly racist against blacks and other minorities? Furthermore, consider the following:

1. Millions of blacks from Africa, the Caribbean, and a variety of countries try daily to come to the United States, even risking their lives to get here.
2. Although Black Lives Matter, Antifa, Liberal Whites and other such groups assert that the United States is racist, none ever make an attempt to leave the United States and move to other countries.
3. Blacks in the United States have gained more wealth than many whites in this country, and all other blacks in other countries.

4. Blacks in America have more freedom than blacks (or whites) anywhere else in the world.

These facts give even more corroboration that the United States is not systemically racist. However, our evidence does not end here as there is additional circumstantial evidence that the United States is not systemically racist. Consider the following racist hoaxes listed below.

On November 26th, 1987, fifteen-year-old Tawanna Brawley, an African American student was found "unconscious and unresponsive" lying in a trash bag a few feet from her apartment in Wappingers Falls, New York, after being missing for four days. The young woman, whose body had been smeared with what appeared to be human feces and clothing being burned and torn, appeared to have been brutally attacked. Written all over her body in charcoal were the words, "nigger", "KKK" and other expletives. She claimed that she had been taken to a wooded area and repeatedly raped by three white males, one of whom she described as a police officer. This case caused an international firestorm and brought together many notables as Al Sharpton, Bill Cosby, Louis Farrakhan and others. Brawley's case began falling apart when a sexual assault kit was administered and came back negative for DNA or other evidence for sexual assault. Also, her body showed no exposure to the elements which is odd for a person being held for several days in the woods, when the temperature had been below zero degrees. Furthermore, the words written on her body had all been written upside down, indicating that she wrote them herself; and the feces found on her body were forensically traced to a neighborhood dog. As a result of all of this the grand jury issued a 170-page report on October 6, 1988, stating that Brawley was probably lying, and that there was no essential evidence that Brawley had been abducted, assaulted, raped, or sodomized.[61]

On March 14, 2006, Durham, North Carolina, police responded to a report of a heavily intoxicated woman who refused to leave her vehicle which was parked in the parking lot of a Kroger Supermarket. It was 1:22 am and when the police arrived, they found 26-yeard old African American, Crystal Mangum, a dancer, stripper, and escort, behaving erratically. Mangum told the officers that she had been pulled into a small bathroom in the lacrosse house and sexually assaulted by at least three male college athletes. In a more detailed version of her account, she stated that she had been suspended in mid-air and ... assaulted by all three of them for a period of at least minutes. Mangum identified three Duke Lacrosse players from a variety of pictures of only lacrosse players, and by Mary 15th 2006 all three players had been indicted on charges of forcible rape, sexual assault, and kidnapping. The News media immediately began vilifying these players and almost 100 hundred Duke professors, the "Group of 88" took out a full-page ad in the local newspaper condemning and attacking the lacrosse players. Mangum case began to fall apart when her dance partner and potential prime witness, Kim Roberts, admitted that there was a short argument that took place at a gathering with some of the players, but no sexual assault took place. Also, a police DNA and a subsequent test did not connect any of the accused lacrosse players to Mangum. The rape charges against the three lacrosse players were dropped on December 22nd, 2006, and the entire case was dismissed.[62]

---

[61] Wilfred Reilly, *Hate Crime Hoax, How the Left is Selling A Fake Race War*, 194-195.
[62] Ibid. 198-201.

In February of 2016, Brian Telfair, African American City Attorney in Petersburg, Virginia told police that between 4:00 and 5:00 p.m. on the 16th, he received a profane and threatening phone call from an unknown male. Using profanity, the caller said that he would kick the rear ends of various city officials, most of whom where black and that he would throw his nigger's rear in the street. Telfair, felt this might be the result of an increase in water bill rates. Because of Telfair's story a meeting among city officials was canceled and Telfair stated the next day that racial slurs and threats of violence against several members of the council had prompted the cancellation. His story began to unravel when Council Clerk Nykesha Johnson told investigators that shortly before the call, Telfair had her purchase a "burner phone" from family dollar. When investigators questioned Telfair, he admitted he had made the phony call himself. [63]

These are just three examples of false racist claims made by blacks against whites, and there are others; but these do not make the country as a whole systemically racist. In fact, the fact that these are phony made-up hoaxes demonstrate that the country is not systemically racist. Because if the country was systemically racist, why would it be necessary to make-up cases of racism? Why not just use one of the many "systemically racist" cases that already exist?

However, the fact that these are made-up hoaxes by the black race against the white race, what some refer to as reverse racism, does not prove systemic racism. But to show that this is not all black against white there are literally hundreds of false white hoaxes against blacks. One common hoax is about white females

---

[63] Ibid. 109-111.

claiming to have been raped by black men. One recent example is as follows:

On March 8, 2017, Teen Breana Harmon, a nineteen-year-old blond, walked into a church along the South Eisenhower Parkway, in Denison, Texas, wearing only a ripped shirt, bra, and panties, with what appeared to be visible cuts and scratches. She claimed that she had been kidnapped from her apartment by three black men wearing ski masks, taken to the woods behind the church, and repeatedly raped. Her case fell apart when she admitted that she had made up the story of being gang-raped. Her confession apparently was sparked by the result of doctors examinations showing no evidence consistent with her claims.[64]

---

[64] Ibid. 240-241.

CHAPTER 6
FACTS YOU NEED TO KNOW

Stand therefore, having girded your waist with truth, having put on the breastplate of righteousness (Ephes. 6:14).

If we are to have a biblical perspective on everything as we are instructed to do in the Scriptures (Phil. 2:5) we must begin by looking for the truth. Truth is that which corresponds to reality and matches its object. Truth is telling it exactly like it is with no embellishments, exaggerations, and omissions and it will always lead you to Jesus. When Pontus Pilate summoned Jesus to come to him, he asked Jesus several questions, one of which was, "Are you a king?" Jesus responded, "You say *rightly* that I am a king. For this cause I was born, and for this cause I have come into the world, that I should bear witness to the truth. Everyone who is of the truth hears My voice." (John 18:33-38). Pilate responded by saying, "What is truth?" then went out to talk to the Jews. Pilate didn't realize that the truth was standing right before Him, even though Jesus had made it very plain. Pilate could've waited for Jesus to answer his question but instead, he made an eternal mistake by turning his back on Jesus and walking away. The truth will always lead you to Christ (John 14:6).

We know however, that it is not often easy to find truth in a culture where there are widespread distortions, exaggerations, and outright lies in the news media, entertainment, sports, academia, politics, and virtually every other area of society. This is one of the reasons why Christians and non-Christians often reach widely different, erroneous conclusions and makes bad decisions on key issues of today, including *Race, Racism, and Slavery.*

This Chapter provides some factual truths about slavery, social movements, politics, and other issues that will help us become more informed when making decisions, plans, determinations, and conclusions regarding *Race, Racism, and Slavery.* Before we get into this factual information, we believe it is helpful to our understanding if we enlighten the reader on two dominant worldviews in our society today, Conservatism and Liberalism.

Conservatism vs Liberalism

As you read through the remaining chapters of this book, we will be referring to conservatives and liberals from time to time as these worldviews play a major part in people who sees and tells the truth about various issues.

Conservatism is a commitment to traditional values and ideas with opposition to change or innovation. Conservatives hold political views that favor free enterprise, private ownership, and socially conservative ideas. They seek to promote a political and social philosophy with traditional social institutions in the context of culture and civilization. Those holding the conservative view generally believe that there is a standard, enduring moral order by which man should live, and many believe that moral order comes from a Creator; that order is made for man, and man is made for it: human nature is a constant, and moral truths are permanent. Thus, they are opposed to change unless that change is done within the framework of that moral order. Conservatives are described as being on the Right. Other terms used for conservatives are "Right-wing," "Traditionalist," "Conventionalist," etc.

Liberalism is a political and moral philosophy originally based on liberty and equality. However, this definition has been stretched to the point where it includes everything but liberty and equality. Those, holding a liberal view will vary on a variety of issues depending on their knowledge, understanding, upbringing, and emotions. Generally, they support issues involving civil rights, democracy, secularism, gender and race equality, internationalism, freedoms of speech, the press, and religion. But this does not mean that their support for these issues is biblically based. In fact, many liberals have been criticized to the point where they've changed their designation as liberals and now prefer to call themselves "progressives" as this will evoke a less negative public reaction than calling themselves "liberal." After all, who can be opposed to "progress?"

In politics, the terms "Progressive" and "Liberal" are generally used synonymously and almost always refer to those who are opposed to maintaining things the way they are, with respect to traditional values, culture, or the institutions of Western civilization (e.g., they want to change free-market economics, republicanism in government, the respected role of churches and religion, etc.). Liberals and progressives are frequently referred to as "Leftists" or those on the Left. Along with the term progressives, Liberals may also be described as "postmodernists," "secularists," "social Darwinists," etc.

Below are various issues and views held by Conservatives and Liberals on each. These views are not held by every person or to the same degree in each category but *general* views. Under each issue, we included the biblical view of that issue.

Views on Race

- Conservatives - Conservatives generally believe that we should live in a color-blind society where every individual is judged on the content of his character and the merits of his actions.
- Liberals – Liberals generally believe that there should be no racial discrimination. However, they do approve of this as long as it primarily benefits minority groups and/or liberal views. (e.g., Affirmative Action).
- Holy Bible – The biblical view on race is that God made all people from one man (Acts 17:26) and Christians are not to go by physical appearance but to look at the heart of an individual (1 Sam. 16:7). We are also instructed in God's Word not to show favoritism or prejudice (1 Tim. 5:21). (Also See Chapter 3).

Views on Abortion

- Conservatives - Conservatives generally believe that abortion ends the life of an innocent child. This includes late-term abortion, infanticide, etc., therefore they generally oppose abortion.
- Liberals – Liberals generally approve the practice of abortion and usually refer to it as "A woman's right to choose."
- Holy Bible – The Bible commands us not to murder (Exo. 20:13) and that we should not take a life of another human because we are made in God's image (Gen. 9:6). The question then becomes, is the fetus a human and when does life begin. While there has been a variety of opinions and views on this, the biblical view is that life begins at conception. For example, the Bible shows that the fetus is a human because the same penalty (death) is prescribed for someone who causes the death of a baby in the womb as for someone who commits murder (Exo. 21:22-25).

We also know that from God's perspective, life begins not just at conception but before conception as He told Jeremiah that He knew him before He formed him in the womb (Jer. 1:5).

Size of Government

- Conservatives – Conservatives generally believe it's important to the future of the country to reduce the size of government, keep taxes low, balance the budget, and get the country out of debt.
- Liberals – Liberals generally believe in big government, big government programs, and higher taxes to pay for social and other programs.
- Holy Bible – Government was established by God (Rom. 13:1-2) for the primary purpose of protecting the rights of its citizens (1 Pet. 2:14, Rom. 13:4). This necessitates a smaller government rather than large governments required by all the other programs and activities in which most governments are involved.

Efficiency of Government

- Conservatives - Conservatives generally believe that government, by its very nature, tends to be inefficient, incompetent, wasteful, and power-hungry. Therefore, a government that governs least, governs best.
- Liberals - Liberals generally believe that the solution to all problems is the government's responsibility. Even when new government programs create new problems, the solution is that another government program will resolve it (e.g., poverty, public schools, immigration, etc.).
- Holy Bible – See Size of Government above.

Gun Control

- Conservatives - Conservatives generally believe that individual Americans have a legal and moral right to use guns to protect themselves and their families.
- Liberals – Liberals generally believe that the Second Amendment right to bear arms should be changed or abolished and certain guns and ammunition should be banned or confiscated from citizens.
- Holy Bible – Scriptures show it is sometimes necessary to be armed for self-defense (Luke 22:35-39). We are also told in the Scriptures to defend our homes and property (Luke 11:21, Exo. 22:2-3). And of course, we are to provide protection for our families and loved ones (Neh. 4:13-14). This requires the use of whatever force is necessary and available to accomplish that purpose. Furthermore, we are told to obey the laws made by man (Rom. 13:1-7). Since the Constitution gives citizens the right to keep and bear arms, having weapons are not violating the law, but taking arms away from law-abiding citizens is violating the law.

Immigration

- Conservatives – Conservatives generally believe that the government should protect its citizens from foreign and domestic intruders and invaders; and that immigrant should only come into the country legally.
- Liberals – Liberals generally believe that anyone who wants to come into the country should be allowed to come, legally or illegally. Some believe that we should have open borders and that Immigration and Customs Enforcement should be abolished.

- Holy Bible – The Bible tells us to treat all immigrants fairly as we would like to be treated (Exo. 12:49; Lev. 19:33-34). This means that since we are to obey the law, immigrants must also obey the law and only enter the country through the legal process.

Views on Capitalism and Socialism

- Conservatives – Conservatives are generally capitalists and believe that entrepreneurs who amass great wealth through their own efforts are good for the country and shouldn't be punished with high taxes or other government takeovers for being successful.
- Liberals - Liberals are generally socialists who view successful business owners as people who cheated the system somehow or got lucky. Generally, they believe wealthy people do not pay enough in taxes, and should give back more for their success.
- Holy Bible – The Bible supports a free-market capitalist system where a person can work, be paid for his work, pay taxes, accumulate wealth, property, etc. For example, God gave private property to Adam (Gen. 2:15-17) and later to the twelve tribes (Gen. 12:7; Gen. 13:14-15). He said that if a man does not work, neither shall he eat (2 Thess. 3:10), meaning, among other things that each capable person is to support himself and not rely on government or other public support.

Love of Country

- Conservatives - Conservatives are generally patriotic, believe that America is a great nation, and are primarily interested in looking out for the good of the country. They believe in "American exceptionalism" and "America first."
- Liberals – Liberals are generally internationalists or globalists. They believe the U.S. is responsible for problems and poor

nations in the world. They also believe that the U.S. is occupier and has taken over other nations.

- Holy Bible – We know from the Scriptures that God blessed the United States with good blessings (James 1:17) for His own purposes. Also, we are to give thanks to God for these blessings (Ephes. 5:20) as He placed us in the nation where He wants us to live (Acts 17:26).

Constitution and Christian Nation

- Conservatives – Conservatives generally believe in God and think that this country has been successful because of God, and that if our country ever turns away from the Lord, it will cease to prosper.
- Liberals – Liberals generally are more hostile to Christianity. This is demonstrated by their dedication to driving reminders of Christianity from society (e.g., 10 commandments, prayer, and Bible reading out of schools and public places).
- Holy Bible – The Bible makes it abundantly clear that if God is the Lord of this nation, we are blessed (Psalm 33:12).

Death Penalty

- Conservatives – Conservatives generally believe in applying the death penalty when appropriate.
- Liberals – Liberals generally do not support the death penalty.
- Holy Bible – The Holy Bible supports the death penalty. "Whoever sheds human blood, by humans shall their blood be shed; for in the image of God has God made mankind (Gen. 9:6). The death penalty is also supported in the New Testament (Rom. 13:1-7; Acts 25:11).

In comparing these two worldviews, it is abundantly clear that the conservative worldview is the closest to adhering to biblical principles. In Christian Ethics, there is a concept referred to as graded absolutism, which basically states that whenever there is a conflict, we go with the view that fits closest to the Scriptures.

Little Known Historical Facts About Slavery

Many Americans today, black and white, hear the word "slavery" and understandably, immediately think of the slave era in the south; and for many, this is how and where slavery started. Democratic Senator Tom Kaine made the following statement from the Senate floor:

"The United States didn't inherit slavery from anybody. We created it."

Indeed, this is the common sentiment among many Americans today who are ignorant of the history of slavery or who are deliberately seeking to deceive those who do not know. A simple review of biblical or secular history will make it abundantly clear that America did not create slavery. Right in the beginning of the Bible, Hebrews were held in slavery in Egypt for at least 400 years (Gen. 15:13). Notwithstanding that, historically, every race, nation, culture, and/or ethnic group has been both slave and master at some point of their existence. Here are just a few examples:

Ancient Greece – Nearly 30% of the population were slaves (thousands of years before America).[65]

Arab Slavers – In the early 1500s black tribes in Africa would raid, capture, and enslave other black tribes, selling them to Islamic Middle East and 'medieval Arabs" into the most degrading forms of slavery.[66]

---

[65] *https://wallbuilders.com/did-america-create-slavery/*
[66] Ibid.

White Slaves – Before the 17th century, a larger number of white Europeans were captured and sold into African slavery than the number of Africans sold into what would become the United States. Just over 300,000 black slaves landed in the North American colonies during this period while there were 1,250,000 white Europeans shipped in slave markets in North America.[67]

Native Americans – Long before Christopher Columbus sailed westward, Native Americans practiced mass slavery with other native Americans which included human sacrifice and cannibalism.[68]

Today, nearly 160 years after America became one of the first nations to abolish slavery, there are currently over 90 nations that do not criminalize slavery. As a result, there are over 40 million people in slavery around the world today, with the highest number being in Africa (approximately 9,240,000). This is almost identical to the total number of slaves brought to North, South, and Central America during 400 years of the Trans-Atlantic slave trade. After all the talk and chaos about America and slavery, it is somewhat ironic that North America currently has the lowest number of slaves.[69]

When most blacks hear "slavery" they inevitably think of the brutal, harsh treatment of African Americans who worked hard in the fields of white slave owners after being kidnapped from their homeland in Africa. This is understandable and some African Americans even view Christianity as a supporter of slavery. It would therefore be helpful if we set the record straight by looking

---

[67] Ibid.
[68] Ibid.
[69] Ibid.

at some aspects of the history of slavery and who was involved in this institution.

One fact about slavery that is seldom mentioned and mostly dismissed is the fact that slaves were owned by blacks, Indians, and other groups as well. Knowing and understanding this fact will help blacks develop a different perspective on the institution of slavery itself. At different times, black slaveowners were found throughout the original 13 colonies and eventually in every slave state.

The first blacks to arrive in Virginia came in 1619 and were indentured servants rather than slaves. An indentured servant is one who signed a contract binding him to work for another for a specified period of time usually in return for payment of travel expenses and maintenance. These blacks worked as indentured servants for a period of time to pay off their debts for traveling to the New World. During the 1850s, a "free negro" by the name of Anthony Johnson owned a 250-acre farm in Virginia with five indentured servants working for him under contract. A black indentured servant by the name of John Casor claimed that his term of service had expired years earlier and Johnson had him working illegally. A 1654 civil court decision concluded that Casor was required to work for Johnson for life. Therefore, one of the first legal slaveowners sanctioned by the court was a black man. [70]

Historian Tiya Miles stated that the number of slaves held by Cherokees were approximately 600 at the start of the 19th century and 1,500 by 1838-9. Various Indian tribes including Creeks,

---

[70] David Emery, *9 Facts About Slavery They Don't Want You to Know*; August 17, 2016.

Choctaws, and Chickasaws held approximately 3,500 slaves at the beginning of the 19th century.[71]

According to historian, R. Halliburton, there were approximately 13.7 free blacks in the United States in 1830, making it a total of 319,599 free blacks. The 1830 census list 3,775 free blacks who owned a total of 12,760 slaves.[72]

Some of the independent slave owners in Africa staged raids on unprotected African villages and kidnapped and enslaved other Africans. Furthermore, there had been a slave trade within Africa prior to the arrival of Europeans. Nevertheless, the European demand for slave mostly in west and central Africa made a significant increase in the number of slaves being taken from their homeland.[73]

Consider these additional facts:

1. Some black slaves were allowed to hold jobs, own businesses, and own real estate.
2. William Ellison was a very wealthy black plantation owner and cotton gin manufacturer living in South Carolina and owned 63 black slaves, making him the largest of the 171 black slaveholders in South Carolina.
3. Brutal black on black slavery was common in Africa for thousands of years.
4. Many slaves brought to America from Africa were purchased from black slave owners.

---

[71] Ibid.
[72] Ibid.
[73] Ibid.

Christianity and the Abolishment of Slavery

Where Christianity stands with slavery in early America, as explained in Chapter four, those who used the Bible to support slavery were distorting the Scriptures and deceiving all who were unaware. Contrary to what many believe, and some teach, Christianity has never supported the institution of slavery as we know slavery in America. As stated earlier, America was established based on biblical principles which means that the Founding Fathers had some degree of morality and respect for human dignity. This is further demonstrated by the fact that not only did America owned less slaves than the rest of the world, but America also led the world in passing anti-slavery laws and abolishment of slavery. During the 400 years of the Atlantic Slave Trade, approximately 12,521,337 Africans were taken to be slaves around the world. Out of this number, only 2.4% (305,326) came to what is now the United States. See Figure 6.1 for the distribution of slaves.[74]

Number of Slaves Received by Various Countries During Atlantic Slave Trade

COUNTRY	NUMBER OF SLAVES	PERCENTAGE
Spain and her Territories	1,061,524	8.5%,
France	1,381,404	11%
Great Britain	3,259,441	26%
Portugal and Brazil	5,848,266	47%
Netherlands	554,336	4.4%

---

[74] *"Trans-Atlantic Slave Trade – Estimates," Slave Voyages,* *https://www.slavevoyages.org/assessment/estimates* (accessed December 6, 2019).

United States	305,326	2.4%
Denmark and Baltics	111,040	0.7%

Figure 6.1

You can see that America took in far less slaves than almost all the other slave-holding nations; and with the exception of Denmark and the Baltics, it received less than all other nations with only 2.4% of the total slaves taken from Africa. If America is to be condemned and vilified because of its slave trade, how much more should these other nations who enslaved far more slaves? Yet, this is not the case as many see the United States today as historically the most racist, prejudice, slave-holding nation in existence. Today, this falsehood is further perpetuated and taught in public schools, colleges, and universities throughout the United States, as well as being reinforced by fake news media. Sadly, many Christians are unaware of these truths.

But America did not just take in less slaves than almost all other nations, because of its Christian origins, America was at the forefront of establishing anti-slavery laws and abolishing slavery. By 1804, over half of the states in America had passed laws abolishing slavery, and this was almost thirty years before William Wilberforce led the effort to transform Great Britain by eradicating slavery and restoring Christian virtues. Because of the biblical beliefs of the early colonies. By 1804, half of America had passed laws for the abolition of slavery and these laws were 99% effective in reaching that goal just six years later. No other nation even came close to accomplishing what the Northern States in America had succeeded in doing.

Presidential approval is not required for an amendment to the Constitution but after the 13th Amendment was approved by Congress, President Abraham Lincoln personally signed it as a symbolic gesture of his strong support. There were thousands of people in attendance and hats were thrown in the air with loud shouts of joy and excitement as jubilation echoed throughout the chambers of Congress. During this period, church services were regularly held at the Capital building and members asked that a sermon be given to honor the event. Who did they ask to deliver the sermon? None other than the Rev. Henry Highland Garnet, the first black to speak in the halls of Congress. His sermon was given on February 12, 1865, and he began by recollecting his own personal experiences with slavery. This, no doubt, had a positive impact on all in attendance because they had just signed into law the first steps to officially ban slavery in America, the 13th Amendment.

Many of the Founding Fathers commented on the institution of slavery in a negative manner:

Thomas Jefferson, at one period in his life stated, "There is preparing I hope, under the auspices of heaven, a way for a total emancipation."[75]

George Washington, near the end of his career said, "It is among my first wishes to see some plan adopted by which slavery in this country shall be abolished by law. I know of but one way by which this can be done, and that is by legislative action; and so far as my vote can go, it shall not be wanting."[76]

Patrick Henry said, "We should transmit to posterity our abhorrence of slavery." [77]

---

[75] David Barton, *American History in Black and White*, 40.
[76] Ibid.
[77] Ibid.

These men were all Christians, among many others who voiced their opposition to the sin of slavery.

Slavery was also denounced by the early Church Fathers, including but not limited to, Augustine, Constantine, Ignatius, Polycarp, Maximus and a variety of other great men of the Christian faith.

William Wilberforce was a British politician who lived a hedonistic lifestyle until his conversion to Christianity. After his conversion, he became resolved to atone for his past lifestyle by making a moral commitment to change the world and make it a better place. Slavery was foremost on his mind, and he took up his campaign in Parliament and in the country, and the "Society for Effecting the Abolition of the Slave Trade" was formed. This Society drew other Christian denominations and Evangelicals, and adopted a rather unique logo featuring a slave kneeling with the words inscribed, "Am I not a Man and a Brother?"

Wilberforce made his first major speech on slavery in Parliament in 1789 where he described the appalling conditions involved in the slave trade. It took many years, and several anti-slavery bills he introduced in the house were defeated but he continued his relentless pursuit to put an end to slavery. The campaign took many years, but gradually accumulated support. Eventually, the Prime Minister, Lord Grenville, introduced a bill to stop the use of British ships to carry men as slaves. It was supported by huge majorities in both houses and passed into law as the Slave Trades Act in 1807. Wilberforce was so touched by the passage of this Act that he wept in Parliament as it passed.

In 1833, a bill to abolish slavery itself throughout the British Empire was introduced. On July 26th, on his deathbed, Wilberforce learned that the government had cleared the way to guarantee its passage, and died three days later, his life's work having been achieved. Here is a follower of Jesus Christ who spent all his Christian life working to put an end to slavery; and God blessed his efforts before calling him home.

Not All About Race

Racism has been and is being used as a weapon to accomplish many goals that have nothing to do with race. It is such a sensitive topic and is so dynamic in its functions that it can be easily manipulated and orchestrated as an excuse or reason to change a program, procedures, systems, society, and even a nation. So, when we look honestly at how racism is used, we can easily see that in most cases, it's not about race at all, but an effort to accomplish some other goal. This is why many people are so quick to label everything as racist. Consider some of the following examples of events and actions taken by using race as the excuse.

Since the killing of George Floyd on May 25, 2020, more than 100 statutes have been toppled, defaced, vandalized and/or removed from various cities and towns throughout the United States. Many, if not most of these statutes, were monuments and images considered to be racist.

Examples include, statutes of George Washington, Thomas Jefferson, General Robert E. Lee, Jefferson Davis, Andrew Jackson, Christopher Columbus, Francis Scott Key, Ulysses S. Grant, Ronald Reagan, and a large number of other confederate monuments, images, and cemeteries. Many of these targets had nothing to do with racism, and many of the men targeted just happened to live during the slave era, although they owned slaves. However, as we've shown, many slave owners did not abuse their slaves but treated them as human beings. Furthermore, we can know that these acts of destruction and accusations had little or nothing to do with racism which is confirmed by the following:

1. On June 30, 2020, the Boston's Art Commission voted to remove a statute of President Abraham Lincoln holding the Emancipation Proclamation while a freed slave rises from a kneeling position with broken shackles on his wrists.
2. President Abraham Lincoln went through great lengths to free the slaves in America and signed the Emancipation Proclamation to get this accomplished. The question then becomes why would the Commission vote to remove a statue of a man who fought against the very system the Commission deemed to be wrong?
3. On July 5, 2020, someone ripped a statue of abolitionist Frederick Douglass from its base in Rochester, New York on the 18th anniversary of the Douglas' famous speech entitled "What to the Slave is the Fourth of July?"
   As mentioned, Frederick Douglass was an abolitionist who spoke and wrote against the institution of slavery. Furthermore, Douglass escaped slavery and became a licensed Methodist preacher. Why would those who oppose racism and slavery toppled his statue?
4. On July 11, 2020, someone set fire to artificial flowers in the hand of a statue of the Virgin Mary at Saint Peter's Parish Church in Dorchester, Massachusetts. The face and upper body of the statue were charred by the flames from the fire.

Even Christianity is being attacked as racist, and according to the Bible, we can expect this to continue (John 15:20). However, as we've seen, Christianity is the religious faith that is against racism and worked to abolish slavery.

When one looks at these events (and there are many others) it becomes painfully obvious that anger against racism and slavery is not the primary motivation for these atrocious acts of violence. Racism and slavery are being used by the enemy as a means to accomplish the broader purpose of causing division and destroying human beings (John 10:10). This is a spiritual problem, and it is important for Christians to understand this which will help us to not develop so much animosity towards those the devil is using.

The fact that racism is stated as the cause for virtually everything shows that racism is not the real problem. Today, virtually everything is considered racist but when everything is racist, nothing is racist. Furthermore, this type of mindset diminishes the impact of real and authentic racism. Blogger Matt Rooney, compiled a list of many objects, events, structures, etc., that are considered racist by those of the Woke movement. (See Chapter 7 for definition of Woke).

1. Classical music
2. Facial recognition technology
3. 'Jingle Bells'
4. The White House
5. Peanut butter and jelly
6. The Washington and Jefferson memorials
7. 'Happy Xmas, War Is Over'
8. The expression "sold down the river"
9. The expression "long time no see"
10. The Declaration of Independence
11. 'The Christmas Song'
12. Star Wars/Darth Vader
13. Peanut galleries
14. Indian sports mascots
15. Voter ID Laws

16. "God Bless America"
17. The National Anthem
18. Police officers
19. Ketchup
20. The legal system
21. Disney's Dumbo
22. The English language
23. Republicans
24. Chopsticks
25. The Gadsden Flag
26. Animal House
27. Opposition to illegal immigration
28. Zoning laws
29. All white men
30. Mark Twain's Adventures of Huckleberry Finn
31. Standardized testing
32. Gucci
33. Prada
34. Buildings named after white men
35. Conservatives
36. City bicycle rentals
37. Dress codes
38. Self-driving cars
39. The United States of America
40. Kellogg's Corn Pops
41. Mathematics
42. The U.S. Constitution
43. Aunt Jemima products
44. Any television shows or movies without a 'major' non-white character
45. Fast food

46. Commercial advertisements featuring fatherless black families
47. Steve Martin's iconic 'King Tut' SNL sketch
48. Pornography
49. Peter Pan
50. The Jungle Book
51. Dr. Seuss books
52. Liquor stores in majority minority neighborhoods
53. The American Flag
54. Betsy Ross's Flag
55. Tipping
56. The expression 'no can do'
57. The Food Pyramid
58. Some pet dogs
59. Most medical physicians
60. Rideshare
61. Grandfather clauses

When we look at this list, it is obvious that all of these have been around for decades and in some cases centuries, so we must ask, "Why all of a sudden are they racist?" Interestingly enough, there were no problems with any of these until the Woke proponents started attacking. And by the way, this list continues to grow.

Conservative Blacks and Racism

If the true problem is how blacks are treated by whites, how do we explain the ever-present disdain by liberal blacks against conservative blacks? Blacks holding a conservative worldview are considered to be "Uncle Toms," "Sell Outs," "Traitors to their Race," and a number of other names that should not be mentioned in public (or anywhere else for that matter).

In 1991, Supreme Court nominee Clarence Thomas, a black conservative thinker, was being vetted for confirmation to a seat on the Supreme Court. Liberals brought in Anita Hill, a black attorney who lodged an 11-hour sexual harassment charge against Thomas, who had been her supervisor. Hill accused Thomas of repeatedly discussing pornography at work, which Thomas denied every one of her accusations. An investigation of the accusation did not confirm Hill's testimony and Thomas was confirmed. Subsequent polls taken showed that Americans believed Thomas by a more than 2-1 margin, and only 26% of women believed Hill's story. Hill was the only woman to have brought up these allegations and many Americans felt that her story did not add up.

What we see here in this situation is a black woman going against a black man, not because of race but because he held a conservative worldview which clashes against the liberal worldview that Hill held. If Thomas had been a liberal, it is highly unlikely that this case would ever been brought to the public, whether true or not. One would think that since everything is about race from the liberal side of the House and Senate, Thomas would have unwavering support from those with this mindset; and would've been confirmed immediately. However, this illustrates that it is not about racism at all, it is a conservative worldview versus a liberal worldview, which means it is a spiritual problem, i.e., the devil is behind it.

Tim Scott, a black Republican from South Carolina, was elected to a full term in the U.S. Senate in 2016. Scott, who holds a conservative worldview is the first black Senator to be elected from the South since 1881 and the first black Senator from South Carolina. In June 2020, Senator Tim Scott introduced his Police Reform Bill which mostly Democrats had argued the need for many months. The bill was carefully drafted by Scott to include many of the Democrats proposals, including, making lynching a federal hate crime, creating a national policing commission to conduct a review of the U.S. criminal justice system; collecting data on use of force by police; barring the use of chokeholds by federal officers, withholding federal funds to state and local law enforcement agencies that do not similarly bar them; and withholding federal money to police departments that fail to report to the Justice Department when no-knock warrants are used. Scott also made it clear to Democrats that he would vote to support some of their Amendments (e.g., defining chokeholds) and that he would, "stay on this floor for as long as it takes and as many amendments as it takes." Scott was willing to work and do what is necessary to get this bill passed.

Despite these concerted efforts and attempts to work with those with opposing worldviews, Democrats voted not to even allow debate on his bill, even though a debate would've given them the opportunities to make changes to the bill. For a bill to become law the House and Senate both pass their own versions then negotiate a compromise that they can give to the President. Since the Democrats control the House, if they still did not like the House-Senate conference, they could still have refused to bring a final bill to the floor. Therefore, they had multiple opportunities to prevent the bill from passing. But instead, they shut the bill down right from the start in the Senate and did not allow it to get to first base. Scott said the Democratic Senators told him, "We're not here to talk about that" and "walked out."

These liberal Democrats obviously do not care for Scott, not because of his race but because of his conservative views. Some of their fellow Democrats and party members have even resorted to calling Scott an "Uncle Tim" a reference to Uncle Tom, a negative term given to blacks who supposedly kowtow to whites and turned their backs on blacks. Little did they know that the real "Uncle Tom" was a minister, author, and abolitionist, named Josiah Henson, born in Charles County, Maryland; was very instrumental in the underground railroad and helped many slaves escape to freedom. The real "Uncle Tom" was a devout Christian who supported his race and helped many slaves even after they were free. This is the Uncle Tom, that Tim Scott represents.

What we see here is mostly liberal white Democrats who frequently complain about racism against blacks, going against a black fellow Senator, not because of his race in which they would normally support but because of their resistance to anyone, black or white, with a conservative worldview, which is closest to the Christian worldview. This is not about race; this is about worldviews. It is the enemy attacking from within the governmental officials, it is a spiritual problem.

Congressional Black Caucus

The foundation for the Congressional Black Caucus (CBC) was started in January 1969 as the Democratic Select Committee by a group of black members of the House of Representatives. In 1971 the organization was renamed the Congressional Black Caucus on a motion made by Congressmen Charles Rangel of New York. According to the CBC's Website, they are committed to "using the full Constitutional power, statutory authority, and financial resources of the federal government to ensure that African Americans and other marginalized communities in the United States have the opportunity to achieve the American Dream." As of 2021, all members of the caucus are part of the Democratic Party.

Byron Donalds, a black conservative Republican was born and raised in the Crown Heights neighborhood of Brooklyn by his single mother. He graduated from High School in 1996 and obtained a Bachelor of Science degree in finance and marketing from Florida State University in 2002. He became a Christian at age 21, elected to Congress in November 2020, and assumed office on January 3, 2021. After attempting to join the CBC, he was snubbed and blocked. As of June 9, 2021, Congressman Donalds has still not been permitted to join the CBC. Donalds stated that "Obviously, the dominant voice in the CBC tends to be Democrat or liberal voices, and I want to bring change to that."

However, it should be noted that the CBC has had Republican members in the past and some Republicans, like Senator Tim Scott made it clear that he has no intention to join the group when offered membership. Conservative Republican Congressman Burgess Owens of Utah, a black man, also stated that he has no plans to join.

Since the CBC stated it is committed to "using the full Constitutional power, statutory authority, and financial resources of the federal government to ensure that African Americans and other marginalized communities in the United States have the opportunity to achieve the American Dream" shouldn't they be interested in the views and concerns of Representatives sent by those African Americans? Here we have a young African American, Byron Donalds, raised in one of the toughest areas of Brooklyn, college graduate with a successful career in finance and marketing, yet he's rejected by the CBC. Clearly, this is not about helping black Americans but furthering a liberal worldview, which in many areas are directly opposed to biblical principles, as we demonstrated in the beginning of this Chapter. In other words, race was used to justify starting the CBC and now the CBC is being used to push a liberal political agenda, an agenda that will ultimately hurt all since it violates biblical principles.

But there is another point that should be considered here. Congress, part of the Legislative Branch of Government is responsible for making the law. The predecessor for CBC was established in 1969 when blacks were fighting for equal civil rights, so it is understandable why such an organization was perhaps necessary. However, today practically all laws that make racial discrimination illegal have already been passed. Why then would racist groups like CBC be allowed in Congress in the first place? Shouldn't it be enough to simply enforce the current racial discrimination laws – laws that were passed to level the playing field for all people, and if enforced, would do just that? Such groups in Congress are unnecessary and as we've seen cause more division than unity. Furthermore, since CBC began in 1969, according to a CNN article, "The typical Black American family is virtually no closer to equal footing with its white peers in terms of income and wealth than it was 50 years ago, when Civil Rights-era reforms were enacted to expand opportunity and limit outright racial discrimination." Since the CBC is "committed to ensure that African Americans and other marginalized communities in the United States have the opportunity to achieve the American Dream" one must agree that they have failed miserably at their job.

Black Lives Matter

The Black Lives Matter (BLM) Movement was started in 2013 by Alicia Garza, Patrisse Cullors, and Opal Tometi after the acquittal of George Zimmerman in the shooting death of Travon Martin in 2012. After the deaths of Michael Brown in Missouri and Eric Garner in New York, the movement gained momentum and grew nationally. It has now established itself as an international movement with organizations in the US, UK, and Canada.

According to the BLM Website their stated mission is to "eradicate white supremacy and build local power to intervene in violence inflicted on Black communities by the state and vigilantes." It is important to note that on BLM's earlier Website it stated, "We disrupt the Western-prescribed nuclear family structure" and "We foster a queer-affirming network" among other anti-biblical principles. While BLM has modified its current Website posts, it has never publicly denounced, repudiated, or disavowed any of its prior views, specifically those mentioned above. It should also be noted that Patrisse Cullors, one of the principle BLM founders was the protégé of Eric Mann, former agitator of the Weather Underground domestic terror organization, and spent years absorbing the Marxist-Leninist ideology that shaped her worldview. She stated in a 2015 video that she and her fellow organizers are "trained Marxists." This clearly sets forth the movement's ideological foundation.

Nevertheless, BLM's title and current stated mission is confusing and questionable at a minimum because the actions and inactions by this organization are diametrically opposite to what their name portrays. They are called "Black Lives Matter" but in many instances, they demonstrate just the opposite. Here are some examples.

Planned Parenthood is the nation's largest abortion provider and has admitted to committing over 4,000,000 post-implantation abortion procedures since it first started in New York State in 1970. A 2020 *Townhall* article reported that Planned Parenthood has located 86 percent of its abortion facilities in or near minority neighborhoods.

According to American Life League, there are approximately 134,850 black babies aborted every year, 369 every day and 15 every second. However, this only includes surgical and medical abortions. These figures do not include chemical abortions which require using drugs that induce or cause abortions (e.g., the morning after pill). One must ask, if black lives matter so much to BLM for them to organize an international movement, why aren't they protesting the placing of hundreds abortion clinics in black neighborhoods and the systematic murdering of hundreds of black babies every day? Don't the lives of these black babies matter?

Black Inner-City Murders

Blacks murdered in inner cities have skyrocketed to astronomical proportions throughout the United States. According to the Daily Caller News Foundation, the percentage of black murder victims in Chicago increased from 70% in 2020 to 81% in 2021. Between January 1, 2020 and June 22, 2020, at least 295 homicides were committed in Chicago, with 207 being black. Between the same period in 2021 at least 317 homicides were committed in Chicago with 257 victims being black.[1]

In addition, many other U.S. cities experienced this same disastrous trend: Consider the following:

Milwaukee – Between Jan. 1, 2020, and June 17, 2020, total homicides increased from 75 to 87 over the same period for 2021. Blacks were the victims of 79 (90%) of the total murders for 2021 and 74% of all murder victims in 2020 (isolated victim data wasn't available for the first six months of 2020).

Pittsburgh – Between January and April 2021, 90% of murder victims were black while during the same period in 2020, 60% were black. There were 20 murders between January and April 2021 and 10 in that same period in 2020. Data beyond April 31, 2021 was not available.

Los Angeles - Between Jan. 1, 2020, and June 21, 2020, blacks were the victims of 92 of the 272 homicides committed in Los Angeles County, which includes the city and surrounding communities. In the same period for 2021 blacks represented 103 of the 315 total homicides. The data showed that the share of black murder victims in the country has stayed level at around 33% year-over-year. However, the uptick in violence for 2021 has caused at least 11 additional deaths in Los Angeles County's black community compared to 2020.

Indianapolis – Blacks represented 58 of the 98 murder victims in Indianapolis between Jan. 1, 2021, and June 1, 2021. In 2020 blacks were the victims in 53 of the city's 70 total murders. While the percentage of homicide victims who were black decreased from 75% to 59% in that period, the number of total black homicide victims still increased.

Baltimore - In Baltimore, black people represented 69 of the 152, or 45%, murder victims between Jan. 1, 2021, and June 17, 2021. While murder statistics between that same period in 2020 were unavailable, black people were the victims of 130, or 39%, of the 335 homicides committed in Baltimore for all of 2020.[1]

The vast majority of these black homicides were committed by other blacks. Since BLM's stated mission is to "eradicate white supremacy and build local power to intervene in violence inflicted on black communities by the state and vigilantes" why isn't there an outcry and action taken by BLM against the "violence inflicted on black communities by state and "vigilantes" in these homicides? Apparently black lives only matter when white cops are involved in the shootings. Perhaps BLM should change their name to "Some Black Lives Matter."

Black Civic Organizations

There are dozens of black civic organizations today whose goal is to help blacks improve their livelihoods in some manner. These include organizations such as The National Association for the Advancement of Colored People (NAACP), the Southern Christian Leadership Conference (SCLC), Black Lives Matter, National Urban League, the National Action Network, Rainbow Coalition, Black Organizers for Leaders and Dignity; African American Planning Commission, and many others – all working to improve the lives of blacks. But how helpful to blacks have they been and how effective are they today? Some of these organizations have been around for many years, while others are relatively younger. Have they improved the lives of blacks? Consider the following:

1. Black men are stuck in poverty more so than other races
2. Black men have lower earnings mobility than whites
3. Black men and women have lower family mobility than whites
4. Blacks have lower marriage rates than other races

In addition to this, blacks have the highest unemployment rates, abortion rates, high school drop-out rates, high crime rates and higher rates with drugs destroying black communities. It appears that these black civic organizations haven't been very effective in improving the lives of blacks, in the past or present. One main reason for this is that these organizations have lost their moral compass (those that had it in the first place) and adopted policies and behaviors that are antibiblical. For example, many, if not all these organizations now support abortion, transgenderism, homosexuality, legalizing drugs, and other behavior that is abominable in the eyes of God. God cannot bless organizations that engage in or support sinful activities as it goes against His holy nature. What all of this shows, however, is that the problems we see is not about race, the problem is spiritual in nature, and spiritual problems must be resolved with spiritual solutions. That solution is Jesus Christ (John 10:10, James 1:17; John 14:6).

CHAPTER 7
CONSEQUENCES FROM FAULTY WORLDVIEWS

Beware lest anyone cheat you through philosophy and empty deceit, according to the tradition of men, according to the basic principles of the world, and not according to Christ (Colossians 2:8).

In this Chapter, we provide various issues that have arisen in recent years within the framework of *Race, Racism, and Slavery.* While all these issues may not directly stem from these three categories, you will find that one or more of these categories provide the foundational base or framework for which they arise. There are many lies, deceit, exaggerations, and distortions of facts fed to us daily, mostly through the news media, public schools, colleges and universities, so it is important that we put forth every effort to detect what is true. As you read through this chapter you will see documented factual information and issues and how using the proper biblical perspective, especially truth, would prevent, mitigate and/or otherwise help resolve these problems.

The Ferguson Effect

The Ferguson Effect is the belief that the increase in violent crime rates in various cities across the country is a direct result of reduced proactive policing. This reduced proactive policing resulted from police officers being charged with brutality, unjustified shootings, and/or other means of inappropriate police behavior. Also, law enforcement officers, especially the police, experience a lack of support from Mayors, Commissioners, and other governmental leaders. As such, police officers began policing only to the bare minimum extent that is absolutely necessary for them to do their jobs. The term Ferguson Effect was coined by St. Louis police Chief Sam Dotson after the shooting of a black man by a white police officer in Ferguson, Missouri, thus the term "Ferguson Effect." The shooting took place as follows:

On August 9, 2014, white police officer, 28-year-old Darren Wilson, fatally shot and killed an 18-year-old black man, Michael Brown in Ferguson, Missouri. With Brown was a 22-year-old friend Dorian Johnson. Officer Wilson said that the altercation began when Brown attacked him in his police vehicle to get control of Wilson's gun. Johnson said that Wilson initiated the altercation by grabbing Brown by the neck, threatening him, and then shooting at him. Both men stated that at this point, Brown and Johnson fled, with Wilson pursuing Brown. Wilson said that Brown stopped and charged at him. Johnson contradicted this statement and stated that Brown turned around with his hands raised after Wilson shot at his back. Johnson stated that Brown shouted, "hands up, don't shoot." Johnson stated that Wilson then shot Brown multiple times until Brown fell. Wilson fired a total of 12 rounds during the altercation, two during the struggle in the car and six-hitting Brown in the front of his body.

This event sparked massive unrest in Ferguson and various cities across the country. A Grand Jury was called and given extensive evidence from the County prosecutor Robert McCulloch but on November 24, 2014, McCulloch announced that the Grand Jury did not find sufficient evidence to indict Wilson. Attorney

General Eric Holder's Department of Justice (DOJ) launched its own investigation and in March 2012, Holder announced that the DOJ did not find sufficient evidence to indict Wilson. Holder's statement from the DOJ in part said the following:

"Though there will be disagreement with the grand jury's decision not to indict, this feeling should not lead to violence. Those who decide to participate in demonstrations should remember the wishes of Michael Brown's parents, who have asked that remembrances of their son be conducted peacefully. It does not honor his memory to engage in violence or looting. In the coming days, it will likewise be important for local law enforcement authorities to respect the rights of demonstrators and deescalate tensions by avoiding excessive displays—and uses—of force."[78]

There were two separate investigations reaching the same basic conclusions about this case. However, if this was not sufficient, in 2020, Westley Bell, a new St. Louis prosecutor, spent five months reviewing the case in an all-out effort to charge Wilson with manslaughter or murder. He too, did not have sufficient evidence and in July, he announced he would not charge Wilson with any crime. In these investigations, it was discovered that the witnesses who incriminated Wilson were found to lack credibility. On the other hand, witnesses who corroborated Wilson were found to have credibility. In other words, those who agreed with Johnson's version of the story were lying while those who agreed with Wilson's version were being honest. The DOJ

---

[78] Department of Justice News Release, *Attorney General Holder Statement on the Conclusion of the Grand Jury Proceeding in the Shooting of Michael Brown*, November 24, 2014.

concluded its findings that Wilson shot Brown in self-defense according to the evidence provided.

Still, the "Hands up don't' shoot" phrase became a rallying cry for BLM and other such radical groups. Communities generally turned against the police and officers were condemned, vilified, attacked, and even murdered in some cities. Police officers began reducing their proactive tactics and resorted to performing their duties only as necessary. As a result, violent crimes in the inner cities began to soar. In October 2015, FBI Director James Comey was speaking at the University of Chicago Law School. He stated in his speech that the likely reason for the rise in violent crime was the drop in proactive policing.[79] In October 2019, at an emergency crime meeting of police chiefs and mayors, Mayor Rahm Emanuel stated that "We have allowed our police department to get fetal."[80]

Speaking of police officers, Mayor Emanuel said, "They have pulled back from the ability to interdict," he said. "They don't want to be a news story themselves; they don't want their career ended early, and it's having an impact."[81]

2015 closed with a 17 percent increase in homicides in the 56 largest cities, a nearly unprecedented one-year spike. Twelve cities with large black populations saw murders rise anywhere from 54 percent in the case of Washington, DC, to 90 percent in Cleveland. Baltimore's per capita murder rate was the highest in its history in 2015.[82]

---

[79] Heather Mac Donald, *The War on Cops*, 2017, 69.
[80] Ibid. 70.
[81] Heather Mac Donald, *The Ferguson Effect, The Washington Post* July 21, 2016.

[82] Ibid.

Robberies also surged in the 81 largest cities in the 12 months after the shooting of Michael Brown in Ferguson, Mo.[83]

In the first quarter of 2016, homicides were up 9 percent and non-fatal shootings up 21 percent in 63 large cities, according to a Major Cities Chiefs Association survey.[84] This is very sad indeed as many lives were lost and others hurt and inconvenienced for the loss of loved ones. Can you imagine the many lives that would've been saved had one person, Dorian Johnson, told the truth from the beginning? All or most of this death are the consequences of not being honest regarding racial issues. But this extends even further as many blacks, including Christians, sometimes refuse to admit the truth based on the evidence in favor of race. The Ferguson case is only one of many where blacks and whites have not told the truth as shown by the evidence or otherwise conjured up false stories claiming racism, as we've shown in Chapter 5.

Defund Police

BLM and many on the Left have called for defunding the police and some have even called for abolishing the police altogether. Several cities have cut funding from police budgets and/or reduced their police force considerably. According to Forbes, at least 13 cities are defunding their police departments as of August 13, 2020. Several other cities are considering the same action as they yield to the demands of radical Leftists and attempt to bring a reckoning to a police system supposedly plagued with systemic racism and police brutality. According to Forbes, Austin, Texas, met with its city Council and voted unanimously to cut $150 million (one third) from its police budget. These funds would

---

[83] Ibid.
[84] Ibid.

then be invested in social programs like food access, violence prevention and abortion.[85]

Seattle voted to cut its budget by $3.5 million. This resulted in the resignation of Seattle first black police Chief, Carmen Best, a 28-year veteran of the Department.[86]

New York cut its 2021 police by $1 billion and reallocated 354 million to mental health, homelessness and education.[87]

Los Angeles cut its police budget by $150 million from a proposed budget of $1.86 billion.[88]

San Francisco approved a $120 million cut to its police and sheriff's department. It promised investments in Black residents, while Oakland passed its own $14.6 million budget reduction.[89]

The nation's capital, Washington, D.C. cut its police budget by $15 million, and the city of Baltimore cut its police by approximately $22 million.[90]

Baltimore eliminated roughly $22 million from its police budget; Portland, Oregon, cut nearly $16 million; Philadelphia $33 million; Hartford, Conn. $1 million; Norman, Oklahoma $865,000; and Salt Lake City reduced its police budget by $5.3 from that previously proposed by the mayor.[91]

According to Democracy Now, Minnesota Congress woman Ilhan Omar says she supports a ballot initiative to abolish the city

---

[85] Jemima McEvoy, *At Least 13 Cities Are Defunding Their Police Departments*, August 13, 2020
[86] Ibid.
[87] Ibid.
[88] Ibid.
[89] Ibid.
[90] Ibid.
[91] Ibid.

of Minneapolis' police department and replace it with a new "Department of Public Safety."[92]

In all these cases, the budgets were apparently reduced as a result of a national response by radical Leftists to defund the police. It must be stated, however, that surveys show that the vast majority of U.S. citizens do not support defunding police or reducing police. A recent Ipsos/USA poll showed that 18% of respondents supported the movement to defund the police and 58% said they opposed it. White Americans (67% and Republicans (84%) were more likely to oppose the movement. However, only 28% of Black Americans and 34% of Democrats were in favor of it.[93] This demonstrates that most Americans do not support defunding the police and there is a relatively small percentage of people driving the entire movement. And rightly so, as we've seen how crime has increased substantially. The FBI has recently reported that murder increased nearly 30% in 2020. The report shows that there were 4,901 more murders committed in 2020 than in 2019, which is the largest single-year increase since the FBI began keeping statistics in 1960. This certainly says much about defunding the police. Furthermore, it is important to understand that law enforcement, including police, were put here by God for our good (Rom. 13:4). Any attack on them is a direct attack on an institution that God has established and an indirect attack on God Himself. Christians should never support destroying an institution that God has established, whether government, police, church or any other entity.

---

[92] Democracy Now, Independent Global News; Rep. *Ilhan Omar Backs Ballot Initiative to Abolish Minneapolis Police & Create New Public Safety Department;* August 5, 2021.
[93] Sarah Elbeshbishi Mabinty Quarshie, *Fewer than 1 in 5 Support 'Defund the Police' Movement, USA TODAY/Ipsos Poll finds,* March 7, 2021.

Critical Race Theory

Critical Race Theory (CRT) is an academic discipline that was formulated as far back as the late 1980s and is built on the foundation of identity Marxism. Hundreds of millions of people have been killed as several regimes underwent Marxist-style revolutions during the 20th century. This includes socialist governments in the Soviet Union, China, Cambodia, Cuba, North Korea, and other governments that murdered their own people. It would help to get a basic background of Marxism to better understand CRT. Marxism is an ideology or political philosophy that focuses on class struggle and various ways to ensure equality of outcome for all people as there should be no rich class and poor class. This includes a political and economic system that abolishes private property (one cannot own private property) and in which all material goods are held in common by all people. This political and economic system was inspired by German Philosopher Karl Marx and his right-hand man, Friedrich Engels. These two set the intellectual framework for the system we know as Marxism today and ultimately communism. Marxism has been tried by many countries in history and has caused the death of millions. It is an atheistic system where a small group controls all means of production and distribution. This small group controls war and peace, who gets rich and who remains poor. They eradicate or fully control every aspect of all institutions, including schools, colleges and universities, private property, and the family. Marxism involves a wide area of thoughts and disciplines, including but not limited to economics, politics, ethics, history, human nature, and religion. All of these must come into play since Marxism's goal is to make certain the outcome is the same for everyone, and they generally exterminate all dissensions from members of the minority class or anyone else they deem to be a problem to their agenda. Their goal is attractive to many as it is marketed by inferring there would be no rich or poor. Everyone would be the same regardless of how much work you put into life. The outcome, however, has always been 100% different. The only ones that end up rich are government officials who are managing the country's money and other assets. True, everyone ends up the same – poor or dead. The understanding of how this happens is simple. If the government guarantees that everyone will have the same regardless of whether one works or not, there is no incentive to work. This means no food and other goods and services necessary for human life are being produced and manufactured. Because food and other goods are scarce, the government then begins to ration food and products per household, starving, frustrated citizens begin to rebel, and the government begins to incarcerate and kill off its citizens. This has happened over and over throughout history for all nations that adopted Marxism. But the primary reason Marxism doesn't work is that it violates biblical principles. A person can sit back, do nothing, and still have the same as the one who has worked hard. God said if an able-bodied person does not work, neither shall he eat (2 Thess. 3:10).

CRT is based on the same foundation as Marxism. Whereas Marxism is an ideology or political philosophy that focuses on class struggle CRT simply replaces "class" with "race." It includes a series of other euphemisms, including "equity," "social justice," "diversity and inclusion," "culturally responsive teaching," and other similar terms and phrases. Critical Race Theorists know that using the terms "Marxism" or "Neo-Marxism" would not go over well with Americans, but a term like "equity" should go over very well since it is easily confused with the term "equality." However, equal opportunity is not the same as equal outcome. Equality refers to everyone having an equal opportunity, while Equity refers to everyone having the same outcome (as in Marxism). The U.S. Constitution, as amended, gives all citizens an equal opportunity. Those who refuse to take those opportunities or fail at those opportunities, for whatever reason, will inevitably have a different outcome. The distinction between these two terms is very different and easily understood. Equality is a principle mentioned in the Declaration of Independence and codified into law in the 14th and 15th Amendments, the Civil Rights Act of 1964, and the Voting Rights Act of 1965. Critical Race Theorists feel all of this is fine, but while it covers nondiscrimination, they feel it provides camouflage for white supremacy, patriarchy, and oppression. Critical Race Theorists want more than this. They want "equality," which, as mentioned, to them means everyone should have the same outcome. For example, to achieve this goal, UCLA Law Professor Cheryl Harris, a proponent of CRT, has proposed suspending private property rights, seizing land and wealth, and redistributing them along racial lines.[94]

CRT itself is a racist ideology as it not only blames all the hardships and grievances of one race to another race; it implies that a black citizen and a white citizen with the same education, same employment, same ideas, and same effort cannot attain similar outcomes because one is white and the other is black. It teaches that being black automatically means being a loser. This is not only a blatant lie but also an affront and insult to all black people to whom this is inferred. This implies that God deliberately made me a loser by making me a black man. With the overwhelming number of blacks who are highly successful in this country, how can anyone ever believe such an outrageous assertion?

---

[94] Christopher F. Rufo, *Critical Race Theory: What It Is and How to Fight It,* Imprimis, Volume 50, Number 5, March 2021.

Furthermore, CRT pushes intergenerational guilt by blaming whites for what their ancestors did in enslaving and persecuting blacks before they were even born. To help us see the ridiculousness in this ideology, honestly ask and answer these questions: Should present-day Germans be blamed and held accountable for the action of Adolph Hitler for the holocaust? Should a Japanese child bear today pay for Hideki Tojo's murder of millions of Japanese? Should a Turkish family be responsible for the Ottoman's behavior when they enslaved hundreds of thousands of Eastern Europeans? If you honestly and accurately answered no to these questions, then you will also know that whites today are not responsible for the enslavement or mistreatment of blacks in history. The Bible shows that children are not to be punished for the sins of their ancestors, but each one is punished for his own sin (Deut. 24:16). Try to imagine your 9-year-old son or daughter being taught in school that he or she can't make it in life because they're black. Conversely, imagine your 9-year-old son or daughter being taught that they are racist because they were born white. You can see how demeaning, denigrating, and evil this is. However, this is what the liberal Left is pushing for in the public school system.

CRT also ignores relevant statistics as more minorities migrate to the United States than any other nation on earth. Many of these minorities thrive and are highly successful after coming to America. Furthermore, according to an article written in The Association of Mature American Citizens magazine, "By wealth, Black, Hispanic and Asian Americans account for 25% of America's millionaires – proving the American Dream, upward mobility, and capitalism. And Pew Research reports most Americans to see racial diversity as good. So much for CRT."[95]

Simply put, CRT makes several basic assumptions:

1. The American government, law, culture, and society are inherently racist in all their structures.
2. Everyone, even those without racist views, perpetuates racism by supporting those racist structures.
3. The race that is oppressed sees their oppression as greater than the actions or intents of the oppressors.
4. The only way to overcome the disadvantages of the oppressed is to uproot and replace the current racial structure.
5. The race that is oppressing will never change out of compassion or consideration for others. They will only change for their own self-benefit.
6. The laws and rights should be applied based on race, not a standard set of laws for everyone.
7. The teaching and training of these falsehoods cause division and is nothing less than pure bigotry. Consider the following examples:[96]

   i.   The U.S. Department of Homeland Security had been telling white employees that they were committing "microinequities" and had been "socialized into oppressor roles."
   ii.   The U.S. Treasury Department, in its training session, told staff members that "virtually all white people contribute to racism" and that they should convert

---

[95] Robert B. Charles, *Critical Race Theory, Seven Hard Truths*, AMAC Vol. 15 Issue 4.
[96] Christopher F. Rufo, *Critical Race Theory: What It Is and How to Fight It*, Imprimis, Volume 50, Number 5, March 2021

everyone in the federal government to the ideology of "antiracism."

iii. The Sandia National Laboratories (responsible for designing America's nuclear arsenal) sent its white male executives to a three-day reeducation camp, where they were told that "white male culture" was analogous to the "KKK," "white supremacists," and "mass killings." The executives were then forced to renounce their "white male privilege" and write letters of apology to fictitious women and people of color.

iv. In Cupertino, California, an elementary school forced first-graders to deconstruct their racial and sexual identities and rank themselves according to their "power and privilege."

v. In Springfield, Missouri, a middle school forced teachers to locate themselves on an "oppression matrix," based on the idea that straight, white, English-speaking Christian males are members of the oppressor class and must atone for their privilege and "covert white supremacy."

vi. In Philadelphia, an elementary school forced fifth-graders to celebrate "Black communism" and stimulated a Black Power rally to free 1960s radical Angela Davis from prison, where she had once been held on charges of murder.

vii. In Seattle, Washington, the school district told white teachers that they are guilty of "spirit murder" against black children and must "bankrupt their thieved inheritance."

There are literally thousands of these examples throughout the United States as CRT permeates every segment of our society from

K-12 to colleges and universities, to federal, local, and state governments, sports and entertainment, and even churches. To judge people by their skin color and/or race is a textbook example of racism, which is precisely what CRT is – Racism. In Dr. Martin Luther King famous 1963 I Have A Dream speech he stated:

"I have a dream that my four little children will one day live in a nation where they will not be judged by the color of their skin but by the content of their character."

Dr. King was referring to his four little children who are black, and blacks have fought to accomplish this dream. Many believe that for blacks, it has been accomplished but isn't it ironic that today many blacks and white liberals are now judging whites by the color of their skin rather than the content of their character. This is certainly not what Christians, black or white, should be doing as we are admonished in the Scriptures to not judge according to how a person looks but to make righteous judgments (John 7:24).

Cancel Culture

The term "Cancel Culture" is frequently used in today's culture and carries negative connotations in its use. It is an attempt to censure or shut someone down in such a way that their voices cannot be heard in public. It is a collective effort to harm the reputation, livelihood, and/or social status of people for violating a particular ideological system or worldview. Cancel Culture proponents use a variety of means to accomplish their goal of harming others including ridicule, lies and exaggerations, getting people fired from their jobs, getting consumers not to purchase their goods and/or services, etc. Some forms of Canceling have always been around but with the advent of the Internet and other Social Media platforms, it is far more prevalent and destructive today. In today's culture, canceling can be for those who are on the "wrong side" or holding the wrong view of anything, including but not limited to the following:[97]

1. Black Lives Matter – A leftist, anti-family, pro-Marxism ideology.
2. Critical Race Theory – Examining society as it relates to race and power.
3. Gender Identity – A person's sense of his or her own gender regardless of biology.
4. Intersectionality – How discrimination and privilege manifest in a person's social framework.
5. LGBTQ – An acronym is symbolizing many sexual deviations.
6. Race/Racism – Discrimination or privilege based on a person's skin color.
7. Sexism – Discrimination of privilege based on a person's sexual orientation.
8. Socialism – Increased governmental oversight with a decrease of personal freedom.
9. Transsexuality – The surgical alteration to change a person's birth sex.
10. White Privilege – The inherent privilege in society due to being white.

The Cancel Culture police will take to Twitter, Facebook, Instagram, YouTube and any other platform or news media to attack anyone who says anything negative or disagrees with the view held by anyone against the beliefs and ideologies on these issues. Consider a few examples that the Left has attacked recently:[98]

---

[97] Matt Slick, CARM, *What is Cancel Culture*, January 5, 2021
[98] Ibid.

1. Pepsi: Criticized for a controversial ad that appropriated global protest movements, including Black Lives Matter.
2. Equinox: The gym club brand faced a backlash after it emerged that its owner was holding a Trump fund-raiser.
3. Starbucks: Was targeted for telling employees not to wear Black Lives Matter T-shirts and badges.
4. Nike: Released a shoe with the original US flag. The flag has only 13 stars and comes from a time when slavery was legal.
5. Uncle Ben's: Changed its name and branding after criticism over racial stereotyping.

These are only some examples of condemnation by the left but there are many cancellations of people, products, and companies for simply saying something deemed inappropriate or not adhering to a politically correct position.[99]

1. A top executive at Boeing recently lost his job because of an article he wrote in 1987 opposing allowing women to serve as fighter pilots.
2. Scarlett Johansson received major backlash in July after discussing actors playing characters of other races, genders, and sexual orientations. She said she should be allowed to play with any person, or any tree, or any animal.
3. Award-winning author of the Harry Potter series, J.K. Rowling, was canceled for tweeting that she supported Maya Forstater, a researcher with a history of making transphobic comments and spreading harmful rhetoric about the "T" community in LGBTQ.
4. There was widespread outcry over the treatment of David Shor, a young data analyst at the progressive group Civis Analytics who was apparently fired for tweeting an academic study about

[99] Ibid.

how violent and nonviolent protests shaped public opinion in the sixties.

5. The fast-food chain Chick-fil-A was canceled by LGBTQ+ activists due to the company's support of anti-LGBTQ+ causes.

Some cancellations, where life-saving information is given, can actually cause the lives of people. As I write, I'm reminded of a team of medical doctors who came together during the height of the COVID-19 pandemic and prepared a video about how they successfully treated some of their patients who carried this virus using a Federal Drug Association (FDA) approved drug hydroxychloroquine. The doctors, by the name of America's Frontline Doctors, made claims that they had used the drug hydroxychloroquine for several of their patients, and their patients were successfully cured of the virus when treated early. Their video was ridiculed and banned from social media platforms almost immediately. Since that time, Dr. Simone Gold, a board-certified emergency physician who appeared in a viral video was also banned from social media for touting the effectiveness of hydroxychloroquine in combating coronavirus. Other physicians and medical personnel met the same fate for supporting this drug. Hydroxychloroquine had been a long-established FDA-approved drug for more than 75 years and is considerably cheaper than other proposed cures for the virus. Furthermore, these doctors claimed to have had proof of the effectiveness of this drug in combating the virus. If they are right, millions of lives could've been saved at a small fraction of the cost being paid by Federal and State Governments today. The FDA-approved drug ivermectin met a similar fate as testimonies demonstrated in its effectiveness in treating COVID was censored. But how would we know if they are right if they are banned from presenting their case? If they are censored? Why would they be banned? Could it be that large pharmaceutical companies did not want to lose the billions of dollars if a cheaper drug was found effective. Since the love of money is the root of all evil (1 Tim. 6:10) this possibility should certainly not be dismissed. The biblical view is to come together and discuss the matter to reach a valid conclusion (Isa. 1:18). Repatriation.

It is not unusual for Democrat politicians to push for reparations around election time as this is a great way to get out black voters. Reparation is money paid or other help or assistance for a wrong done in the past. Reparations for slavery is a concept that victims of slavery and/or their descendants should be recompensed or compensated in some manner for the wrong afflicted upon them. In some cases, in the past, reparations have been given voluntarily by individuals and institutions and can take numerous forms, including but not limited to monetary payments, scholarships, waiving of fees, land, apologies, renaming a street after someone, etc. There are also examples of international reparations for slavery, but these only included instances of the official recognition of the injustice imposed upon slaves and apologies, but there was no monetary compensation.

Slavery of course officially ended in the United States in1865 with the 13th Amendment to the Constitution, which stated in part, "

"Neither slavery nor involuntary servitude, except as a punishment for crime whereof the party shall have been duly convicted, shall exist within the United States, or any place subject to their jurisdiction."

At that time, approximately four million African Americans were officially set free, and that was the end of legalized slavery in America. Since that time, up until this very day, there has been a call for repatriation, although recently this is more of a talking point because, as we will see, most Americans do not support reparations and there are many problems that such an attempt would incur. Nevertheless, there is some support and has been some concerted effort to make repatriation a reality.

Former Congressman John Conyers of Michigan reintroduced a bill entitled the "Commission to Study Reparation Proposals for African Americans Act" every year from 1989 until he resigned in 2017. On July 30, 2008, Congress passed a resolution apologizing for American slavery and subsequent discriminatory laws. Also, the following nine states have officially apologized for their involvement in the enslavement of Africans.

- Alabama
- Connecticut
- Delaware
- Florida
- Maryland
- New Jersey
- North Carolina
- Tennessee
- Virginia

This is a form of reparations, as stated above but as can be expected, most people who support reparations prefer monetary compensation. However, such a measure would present insurmountable obstacles and complications that could not be easily or effectively overcome, as shown below.

In 2014 *YouGov* conducted a study that showed only 37% of Americans believe that slaves should have been provided compensation in the form of cash after being freed. Also, only 15%

believed that descendants of slaves should receive cash payments. The findings in this study indicated a substantial divide between black and white Americans on this issue. It showed that "Only 6% of white Americans support cash payments to the descendants of slaves, compared to 59% of black Americans. Similarly, only 19% of whites – and 63% of blacks – support special education and job training programs for the descendants of slaves."[100] National Review writer Kevin D. Williamson wrote in his article "The Case for Reparations" "The people to whom reparations are owed are long dead."[101]

There are many problems in implementing a repatriation project for African American descendants of slaves. First, how do you identify who is an African American? Would that include someone who is 10%, 20%, 40% African American? Should the one-drop rule be used in making this determination?[102] Should you prorate reparations based on DNA analysis? How do you deal with people like Barack Obama, who have no relatives directly in America who were slaves? What about people like Kamala Harris whose father said that as the Caribbean, his family-owned slaves? What about the Irish, Hispanics, and others who were slaves but not African Americans? Should they make claims? How do you determine the amount of compensation each should receive? Where would the money come from? How do you justify using

---

[100] Peter Moore, *Overwhelming opposition to reparations for slavery and Jim Crow*, June 2, 2014.

[101] Kevin D. Williamson, *The Case for Reparations*, May 24, 2014).

[102] Because defining "black" was next to impossible, whites came up with a standard which said if an individual had one drop of black blood, that individual was officially black. This rule was codified into law and could be found on all legal and official documents such as birth records, marriage licenses, census forms, etc. see, "An Act to Preserve Racial Integrity." *https://versounmondonuovo.wordpress.com/tag/act-to-preserve-racial-integrity/ for additional information.*

today's taxpayers' money for repatriation since slavery was in the past? Should a white carpenter in Omaha, Nebraska, earning $40,000 per year pay compensation to a black billionaire like Oprah Winfrey? One economist estimates that a fair reparation value would be anywhere between $1.4 to $4.7 trillion or approximately $142,000 (equivalent to $155,000 in 2020) for every black American living today. The U.S. currently has a national debt approaching $30 trillion. Should trillions more be added to the national debt (which will affect all future generations) of the U.S. Treasury?

As you can see attempts to initiate a repatriation project involve many challenges and these are just some of them. Other problems that are not as easily seen are psychological, anger, jealousy, people quitting jobs, etc. Some sins of the past leave an indelible impact on society and cannot be corrected by humans, only repented of. Jesus will resolve all such problems at His Second Coming and setting up His Kingdom (Rev. 21:4).

Some Christians have argued for repatriation to descendants of slaves with what they believe to be biblical support. Some have pointed to the following passage of Scripture to show that repatriation is indeed biblical:

You shall not make for yourself a carved image—any likeness of anything that is in heaven above, or that is in the earth beneath, or that is in the water under the earth; 9 you shall not bow down to them nor serve them. For I, the Lord your God, am a jealous God, visiting the iniquity of the fathers upon the children to the third and fourth generations of those who hate Me, 10 but showing mercy to thousands, to those who love Me and keep My commandments (Deut. 5:8-10).

Some Christians argue that this passage of Scripture shows that successive generations bear the guilt for the sins of their ancestors but this is not what this passage is teaching us. At first read, this may seem like a possibility, but closer analysis of these verses makes it clear that this is not the case. This passage talks about idolatry a carved image, and says that pursuing idolatry will have long-term effects on subsequent generations. It helps to understand that there are *long-term effects* of sin and *judicial guilt* for sin. Descendants do not bear the guilt for their ancestor's idolatry but they will feel the effects of it. We see a similar situation of this when David committed adultery with Bathsheba and had her husband Uriah killed, he lost his kingdom, and the loss of his kingdom affected subsequent generations of his family for a long time. His children suffered the effects of David's sins, but they were not judicially guilty for his sins. Likewise, whites today feel the effects of their ancestor's sins but they are not judicially guilty for their ancestor's sins. Ancestral guilt is not taught anywhere in the Bible, Old or New Testament.

Wokeness

Wokeness is a term that comes out of the CRT family of words, which itself stems from racism. To be "woke" is to be aware of the racial problems in society. Theology Professor Owen Strachan provided an excellent definition of Wokeness in his book *Christianity and Wokeness*. Wokeness, he stated is:

"The state of being consciously aware of and "awake" to the hidden, race-based injustices that pervade all of American society;

this term has also been expanded to refer to the state of being "awake" to injustices that are gender-based, class-based, etc."[103]

In other words, to be woke, one must be continuously aware of all the racism that is rooted in every aspect of our society, including art, business, government, public schools, colleges and universities, sports and entertainment, laws, politics, the Constitution, as well as a certain class, specifically Whites or Caucasian. Woke proponents believe that because of racial privilege, all society is considered to be structured with a racist foundation, including anyone who supports or participates in any part of this society. Systemic racism or structural racism are two of the terms frequently used to describe this condition of racial inequity and only whites can win this game. To defeat such a system the attack must be on those who created it - whites.

In a 2016 training video, a speaker by the name of Ashleigh Shackelford spoke before an audience of women, many of whom were white, and said that "all white people are racists; she stated that they had no hope of changing, "No, you're always going to be racist, actually...Even when you're on a path to be a better human being."

To say, "all white people are racists' is about as arrogant and self-righteous as one can get. Furthermore, any thinking person who is honest can immediately see that such a broad, generic statement is clearly untrue. But this is an example of the type of teaching and training that is going on in various organizations and institutions throughout the United States as this video went viral. Those who have been victims of racism in the past have now become racists themselves. What Shackelford did was pushed a

---

[103] Owen Strachan, *Christianity and Wokeness*, 213, Good News Publishing, 2021.

false ideology in an effort to get everyone "woke" and to adopt her racist worldview. The proponents of CRT and wokeness believe that there is no middle ground between encouraging racism and fighting racism, there is only antiracism. Stated differently, the only way to effectively end racism is to become an antiracist and defeat "whiteness."

To become an antiracist, one must commit to making a total and complete personal social revolution. The antiracist must take aggressive and deliberate action to make sure the entire "white supremacy" system falls. To accomplish this, some of their proposals are: [104]

1. Reparations for descendants of slaves
2. Restructuring hiring practices to ensure diverse personnel
3. Protesting and opposing, even violently, if necessary, stubbornly "racist" entities and individuals
4. Reeducating youth to show the systemic wickedness of America as a country
5. Practicing "lament" and the personal confession of one's inherent racism (especially if "white")
6. Performing public acts of secular repentance to right wrongs, and
7. The destruction at every turn of "white supremacy" anywhere it can be found.

Each of these proposals and/or the manner in which they are to be executed violate biblical principles, meaning as followers of Jesus Christ, Christians should not be involved in these initiatives or even hold these views (Phil. 2:5).

---

[104] Ibid. 14.

Hurting Those it Claims to Help

Sadly, the Woke crowd is hurting and destroying the very people it proposes to be helping, blacks and other minorities. For example, the State of Georgia revised its voting laws because of improprieties in the 2016 election. The Georgia law was revised in such a manner as to make it easier for its citizens to vote but more difficult to cheat. As a result of the change in this law, which Woke proponents deemed to be racist, Major-League Baseball (MLB) Commissioner Rob Manfred made the announcement to move the 2020 All Star Game from Atlanta to Denver. This was done to stand up for blacks whom they believed to be hurt by the election reform legislation, and to punish those who were involved in making those legislative voting changes.

However, the results were the exact opposite. While Atlanta is 51% black, Denver is only 9% black and 76% white, meaning a severe economic blow was delivered to black-owned businesses by moving the game to Denver from Atlanta. Approximately 30% of the businesses in Atlanta are black owned so black businesses and residents were hurt by this action taken by MLB.

Another example of wokeness hurting those it claims to help is with President Lyndon Baines Johnson's 1960s Great Society and War on Poverty programs (note that Wokeness has been around for decades but only recently given the name). This program has been a monumental failure that has crippled blacks economically, financially, socially, and morally and left them in poverty in greater numbers than ever before. These social programs did little more than incentivized people not to work and have resulted in a black community that is largely dysfunctional, especially in the inner cities with high crime rates, drugs, teenage pregnancies, single-family households and soaring high-school dropout rates. All of this has brought about a serious negative impact on the very people whose lives they promised to improve. There are people that legitimately needed this help but from my personal observation, there were far more abusing the system, both from the side of the government and the recipients of these social programs. The reason we see these dreadful unintended consequences is because such social programs are diametrically opposite to what the Bible teaches, which is that every able-bodied person should work (2 Thess. 3:10).

Defunding the police was a movement that supposedly would help blacks and other minorities by eliminating or reducing police brutality on blacks and other minorities. Since this movement began, crime has skyrocketed, primarily in the black communities, the people they claimed it would help. See above for details.

There are many other ways Wokeness is hurting the very people it claims to help, including, for example, indoctrinating blacks into believing they're the victims of racism, and therefore they can't succeed, putting forth efforts to eliminate chartered schools, ending school programs for gifted and talented kids, dumbing down advanced courses so blacks can keep up, not arresting and prosecuting blacks for crimes committed, etc.

But the greatest overall problem with the Woke movement is that it is antibiblical in its very nature because, among other problems, it distorts and hides the truth. As we stated in Chapter 1, truth is foundational for every solution and must be searched for and adhered to since Jesus Christ is the answer to everything. When you go against the Bible or violate biblical principles, you're going against Jesus, and from there, all problems arise. Truth is absolute, which means it is true for all people, at all times, in all places and the truth always leads you to Jesus Christ (John 14:6) and sets you free from sin and other burdens (John 8:32). When people are taught that truth is what you believe it to be or how you see it to be, this is called relativism and is an outright lie. When children are taught that if they feel they are a male, even though they were born female, or when children are taught that $2 + 2 = 5$, or any other number they think it should be, it is nothing less than harmful indoctrination and child abuse. Wokeness teaches that the United States is systematically racist, and all white people are racist. Both are outrageous lies, as we've already demonstrated.

1619 Project

In August 2019, just in time for the 400th anniversary of the arrival of the first enslaved Africans in the colony of Virginia, writers from the *New York Times* published a document currently referred to as the 1619 Project. This was a series of essays and articles written with the goal of rewriting America's history. According to The New York Times Website, the intent of this Project is "to reframe the country's history, understanding 1619 as our true founding, and placing the consequences of slavery and the contributions of black Americans at the very center of the story we tell ourselves about who we are."

The opinions expressed in this project touched nerves, brought about outrage, and initiated debate among those in American historical and political scholarship throughout the country. The main thesis of the project was that the true beginning of America was 1619 and not 1776, as had been taught in public schools since their inception. The writers' assertion was that 1619 was the year when the first African slaves arrived in America at Jamestown, thus being the true beginning of America. Numerous historians have rejected this project for containing an erroneous view of history, is not a work of historical scholarship, and is nothing but leftist political propaganda. Dr. Lucas Morel, Professor of Politics at Washington and Lee University, made the following observations of the Project:[105]

- The study of slavery's impact on economic life is critical to understanding how slavery affected the economic development and character of American capitalism.
- However, 1619 is a political project riddled with factual errors, and its theories on capitalism should not be conflated as an accurate historical account.
- Only complete and accurate histories belong in classroom curricula, and thus, the 1619 Project must not be taught as history in our schools.

We can easily understand Morel's point as we read through some of the other ridiculous assertions made in this document. We've listed three of them with a short rebuttal to each.[1]

1. **Preserving slavery was the real cause of the American Revolution. Independence from England was nothing but a smokescreen.**

This is completely false. History shows that the institution of slavery in America was not under threat from the British at the time of the American Revolutionary War. In fact, the British did not free their own slaves until 1833, and this was 57 years after the Declaration of Independence in America. In other words, Britain was supporting the institution of slavery before the American Revolutionary War started, during the war, and for 57 years after the war ended. The American Revolutionary War was fought for a

---

[105] Lucas E. Morel, *A Review of the 1619 Project Curriculum*, December 15, 2020.

series of events including, but not limited to, America wanted its own independence and to operate as a sovereign nation, high taxes levied on the Colonies to help pay for the French and Indian War, and a variety of acts that were passed by the British but deemed to be intolerable to the Colonies. There were a variety of other reasons for the Revolutionary War but maintaining slavery was certainly not one of them.

2. Slavery made America rich.

Some Americans got rich because of slavery, but America itself did not get rich from slavery. In fact, it was almost the opposite as the institution of slavery placed an enormous economic drain on America. In 1860, the South had only one-sixth as many factories as the north, and almost 90% of skilled, well-paid professionals were based in the north. Banking, railroads, manufactories were all in the north. Furthermore, the cost of abolishing slavery was enormous. After the civil war was fought, much of the south was destroyed and decimated. Farms and plantations were burned down, and crops were destroyed, leaving the south in a substandard economic situation. It was so bad that The Reconstruction (a period of rebuilding the South after the Civil War) lasted 12 years, from 1865 to 1877. Lincoln borrowed billions to pay for abolishing slavery, and thousands of human lives were lost. 360,000 union soldiers died to free 4 million slaves from slavery. In almost 200 years since the civil war, the population has grown almost 900% and the GDP has increased almost 12,000%. So to say that slavery made America rich is ludicrous.

3. Racism is an Unchanging Part of America

This is also a ridiculous claim as America is a land of opportunity for everyone as is evidenced by millions of blacks and other minorities of all colors have been highly successful in this country. See Chapter 5 for greater details on this topic.

As we've seen, the 1619 project is racist from the beginning, completely inaccurate, and just another effort by the enemy to divide and destroy men, women, boys and girls in this country by pitting them against each other. Keep in mind that we are looking at this (and all other subjects in this book) from a biblical perspective.

CHAPTER 8
RACISM, LIBERALISM, WOKENESS, AND THE CHURCH

"And I also say to you that you are Peter, and on this rock, I will build My church, and the gates of Hades shall not prevail against it." (Matt. 16:18).

Before going into how the church has been affected by racism, liberalism, and wokeness, we believe it is best to give a brief overview of the origin and purpose of the Church.

Origin and Purpose of the Church

The word "church" comes from the Greek word, *ekklesia* and it means "called out ones" or in Christian circles, it means those who have been called by God through His Son Jesus Christ. And of course, there is the concept of the visible church and the invisible church. The visible church consists of those whom we see going to a place of worship each weekend, usually Sunday. Even though they may attend a worship service every weekend, if they are not indwelt by God's Holy Spirit, they are not a part of the true body of Christ (Rom. 8:9). The invisible church consists of only those whom God has called, have repented of their sins, accepted Jesus as their lord and Savior, and who are indwelt by the Holy Spirit. As such, the church is not the building itself, although we commonly use the term to refer to the building where Christians meet to worship God. The Church was started by Jesus Christ approximately 2000 years ago and Jesus is the head of the Church (Col. 1:18).

The Church serves a variety of purposes (worshipping, communion, learning, fellowshipping, serving, praying, witnessing, encouraging, inspiring, uplifting, etc.) but the overall purposes of the Church can be summed up into three categories:

Worship God

We read in the Scriptures that Jesus said His Father is looking for worshippers (John 4:23) and that worshipping God is one of the supreme purposes for which we were created (Phil. 2:9-11; Psalm 29:1–2). Jesus started His church and provided us a sanctuary to come together to worship God (Heb. 10:25). We worship God because we recognize that there is no other being, pursuit, pleasure, or anything else that is worthy of worship. The church is one of the ways we come together, meet with God and praise Him for His goodness, love, mercy, grace, holiness, beauty and all that He is.

Feed the Flock

Feeding the flock, that is, coming together to learn all we can about God is another broad category for the purpose of the church. We are told to "Grow in grace and knowledge of our Lord and Savior, Jesus Christ (2 Pet. 3:18)." Speaking of the Apostles, we read, "They devoted themselves to the apostles' teaching and to fellowship, to the breaking of bread and to prayer." (Acts 2:42, NIV). Here we see that another purpose for the church is to teach biblical doctrine (along with fellowshipping, observing the Lord's supper, and praying, which is a form of worship). An important point that must be observed here is that they were *devoted to*

171

teaching biblical doctrine. This means that the church is to stick to the Bible in its teaching and not deviate from the Scriptures.

Evangelize Others

The third category for the purpose of the church is to fulfill the Great Commission as Jesus commanded (Matt. 28:18-20). This means that we are to faithfully represent God by walking in the Spirit and allowing God to use us to glorify Him and be a blessing to other (1 Cor. 10:31-33). It means that we are to be ready to give an answer for the hope that is within us with gentleness and respect that we might win others for Jesus Christ (1 Pet. 3:15). We should be ready to witness to friends, family, neighbors, coworkers, fellow students, and anyone else whom God places in our paths.

So, we can see that the three primary purposes for the church is to (1) worship God, (2), feed the flock i.e., teaching and preaching, and (3) evangelize others, i.e., those who have not accepted the saving grace of Jesus Christ and the gospel. As we go through this Chapter, we will see that many churches have incorporated other social issues into their programs and teachings, which have caused the gospel to be watered down and/or disregarded in their teachings. Since the Bible has a perspective on everything, it is appropriate to speak on social and other issues, but this should always be done from a biblical perspective, i.e., what the Bible has to say about the particular issue being addressed.

How it all Began

Racism/liberalism/wokeness ideology is very similar in that it has its foundation in Marxism and was perpetuated by liberal college professors who taught this ideology in college and university classrooms. This teaching was not limited to philosophy, psychology, or history but was used as a foundation for almost every other academic discipline in the school's curriculum. It was worked into the framework of virtually all courses in every program, curriculum, and this is facilitated by the fact that they have labeled everything as racist. So regardless of one's specialty in college, they are trained to see everything through a racist lens. Many of the students under these professors and instructors, upon graduating, became teachers, politicians, and leaders in various civic organizations. As such, this ideology became part of the public school system, government, business, community and is currently infiltrating the church. We've seen in Chapter 7 how various government agencies and public schools are providing employees with "awareness training" which is another name for racism/liberalism/wokeness training.

Ibram X. Kendi is a highly praised black professor and antiracist activist at Boston University. In July 2020, he took the position of Director of the Center for Antiracist Research, and in 2016 he published a best-selling book entitled, *Stamped from the Beginning,* and after the death of George Floyd in 2020, he published another book entitled *How to Be An Antiracist.* This book sold a substantial number of copies and included sales to various institutions like public schools, governmental agencies, and professional groups, all wanting to learn about racial unrest and how to become an antiracist. His work has been endorsed by the federal bureaucracy, the US military, and many fortune 500 companies, never mind that these are all large power structures that Kendi claims to oppose. Needless to say, his liberal, woke worldview is antibiblical and should be rejected by all who are followers of Jesus Christ. Notice some of his statements and views: I include in parenthesis the biblical perspective after each comment for your edification.

"When I see racial disparities, I see racism," (What about listening to the other side to see if there are other explanations? Prov. 18:17)

"The life of racism cannot be separated from the life of capitalism," he says. "In order to truly be antiracist, you also have to truly be anti-capitalist." (The Bible supports free-market capitalism, see Chapter 6).

He proposes "defunding the police" and restricting free speech. (Both of these are anti-biblical for policemen were established by God (Rom. 13:1-4).

Racism is "A collection of racist policies that lead to racial inequity that are substantiated by racist ideas." (This definition does not define racism as it uses the word three times in its definition, this is a double talk which is characteristic of an unstable man. James 1:8).

He argues that "The only remedy to past discrimination is present discrimination." (Since when do you fight evil with evil? We are to repay evil with good, 1 Pet 3:9)

He proposes a federal "Department of Antiracism," to suppress "racist ideas" and veto, nullify, or abolish any law at any level of government not deemed "antiracist" unaccountable to voters or legislators. (This is how socialist, communist, and totalitarian government functions. Government was established by God to protect the rights of its people. Rom. 13:1-4; and supports the capitalist form of government, see Chapter 6).

The Black Church

When we look at the history of the black church it is easy to see how the racist/liberalist/wokeness ideology came into the church. From the beginning, the African American church, has been not only a place of worship but served as a refuge for blacks for a variety of other reasons. Dr. Henry Louis Gates stated that the black church has two major stories. Gates stated:

"To be sure there is no single Black Church, just as there is no single Black religion but the traditions and faith that fall under the umbrella of African American religion, particularly Christianity, constitute two stories: one of a people defining themselves in the presence of a higher power and the other of their journey for freedom and equality in a land where power itself – and even humanity – for so long was (and still is) denied them. Collectively, these churches make up the oldest institution created and controlled by African Americans, and they are more than simply places of worship."

The Black Church served a multifunctional purpose, along with worship. It was a place that addressed social, racial, economic, political, psychological, educational, and every other need of blacks, slave and free. It was a place where blacks would meet to discuss the racial and cultural problems and it has a language of its own, music of its own, preaching of its own, and worship of its own. This tradition carried on to this very day where all needs of blacks from teaching kids reading and arithmetic to helping adults with registration and voting drives. This was all brought about as a result of slavery and racism, because no other civic or social institutions were open to them, so blacks had to turn to the church for practically everything. At the highest level, the black church functions as a spiritual center where blacks worshipped God and heard sermons while all of the other aforementioned services were secondary. However, as the population grew, the black church grew, racial and political issues became more prevalent, and it was not long before slave theology gave rise to black activism. And as racial and political issues became more prevalent, like all other institutions, many, if not most of the black churches became more political, and began placing more and more emphasis on social, political, and racial issues, and the racist/liberal/wokeness ideology began to take a greater role in the church in terms of sermons, Bible studies, and fellowshipping events. Consider the examples set forth below:

Urbana Student Missions Conference has been holding Christian Conferences each year since its first in Toronto, Canada in 1946. Since 2006 the conferences were held in St. Louis, Missouri. It brings together a "diverse mix of college and graduate students, faculty, recent graduates, pastors, church and ministry leaders, missions organizations and schools." Its conference Director is Stacey Woods who envisioned the conference as "just the beginning of a mighty missionary movement ... an instrument in God's hands, not only as a home mission, preaching the Gospel to America's college students, but also as ... a pool of consecrated manpower for the evangelization of the world." This is an excellent movement and a great vision indeed. There have been great Christian speakers at these conferences in the past, including the likes of Billy Graham, John Stott, and Elisabeth Elliot. However, in 2015, a young black lady by the name of Michelle Higgins spoke and gave a completely difference turn to the type of messages these Christians were accustomed to hearing. Higgins included in her speech the following:

"Do you see that racism is the age-old idol in our closet that we can't manage to tear down? Do you see it in our houses of worship, my brothers and sisters, right beside the little sexism idol and the classism idol and the cool-car idol and the good-job idol and the college-degree idol? Do you see it? Tear it down and admit, with torn shirt, ash in our hair, on our hands and knees, 'Oh God, we have committed adultery with white supremacy!' The

176

evangelical church has taken the dominance and power of Eurocentrism and made it its side-piece or part-time lover. Maybe we haven't been convinced that white-supremacy is our idol, is our little god, but we do know that we have all of the techniques, all of the people that we need to eliminate both racial and class-based injustice on the continent. We have all we need except the will to do it, and that may be because we're so comfortable that we don't want to change. That may be that I'm so comfortable with my wonderful, high-class dentist, I don't want to pay for somebody to get some good teeth."

Her speech was really an introduction of woke Christianity in the church. These students and faculty in attendance were no doubt shocked and surprised by a message of accusation and division instead of unity, love, and inspiration. She accused the audience of "adultery" with "white supremacy" without even knowing who was in the audience. In other words, her views were just like Ashleigh Shackelford, Ibram Kendi, and other woke proponents - all white people are automatically racist by virtue of being white. It's worth noting that she didn't include herself in her racist accusations since only whites can be racist, from the woke proponents view, whether in or out of the church.

In the late 1990s, two sociology professors, Michael O. Emerson and Christian Smith conducted a joint study on issues involving race in the church and evangelicalism. Their research was carried out through a nationwide telephone survey of 2,000 people and 200 face-to-face interviews. They included the results of their study in a book entitled *Divided by Faith* which was published in September, 2001 and landed at the top of the Gospel Coalition's (TGC) 2016 recommended reading list on the topic of racial division. They argue that whites and blacks should work together to "recognize" and "resist" racialized structures of inequalities. Their contention is that although slavery, Jim Crow laws and legal segregation are no longer realities in America, racism has not declined. Racism is not as obvious but is more covert and vast inequalities exist in the areas of income, employment, health care and others, all can be attributed to systemic racial injustice. Furthermore, all white evangelicals are complicit in these racial injustices because they support the American system and enjoy its fruits. To combat this racial injustice, whites, who are the main creators and benefactors of this systemic racism must repent of their personal, historic, and social sins. If these social sins are not confessed and overcome, they will be passed on to future generation, thereby perpetuating the racialized system, thereby perpetuating sin.

Their recommendation and contentions are ripe with woke thinking right from the beginning. When they speak of working together to "recognize" and "resist" racialized structures, this means identifying what is racist, but the problem is, everything they see is racist, and all white people are racist. Why must I go searching for something that is wrong or evil? If people are looking, digging, and searching for something that can be called racist, because they want to satisfy their goal, they will ultimately end up labeling things as racist, which are not actually racist. But taking this action is racist within itself. If one is looking for trouble, he will find it and this is exactly what this racist/liberal/ideology does. Secondly, why would we ask someone to repent of something their ancestors or friends did? There is nowhere in the New Testament where Christ or His Apostles ever ask anyone to repent of a sin committed by a family member. No one is considered guilty of a crime their ancestor committed, so why would we try to force them to repent of it? It is more than enough for us to repent of our own sins much less someone else's.

This kind of racist/liberation/woke thinking has gotten into the Church and is causing nothing but division among the brethren; or at the very least preventing the love and unity that we are to have for each other (John 13:34).

In 2003, Daniel Hill, a Caucasian, followed his vision and built a multicultural church to transform the city of Chicago through worship reconciliation, and neighborhood development. In 2017, Pastor Daniel wrote a book entitled *White Awake*. In his book, he explained his personal journey of being spiritually blind to white supremacy early in his ministry to the point of being painfully awakened. He asserts that all white people are racist whether they are aware of it or not; and that the "primary enemy of God's kingdom in this realm is white supremacy." He further stated the following:

"I repent all the time because I believe I'm surrounded by the sickness of racism. I see the sickness in the ideology of white supremacy and have no doubt that it has infected me ... I see the sickness of systemic racism and have no doubt that I contribute to it in ways I'm not aware of, I'm surrounded by sickness, and I am sick."

Pastor Daniel focuses on white supremacy as being the primary enemy of God's kingdom. Historically, white supremacy referred to racial superiority by advocates of race-based segregation, including movements as the KKK, Skin Heads, and alt-right pro-Aryan groups. Today, white supremacy includes everyone who is white and/or have political views different from those making the claims. Woke proponents today see white supremacy as a condition possessed by all white people and that whites are automatically the superior race, whether they are aware of it or not, and all other ethnicities are inferior to them. As a result of this kind of woke thinking, Pastor Daniel is certain that he is a racist, but he can't determine what it is that he is doing that is racist. He feels that he's just a racist by nature so he agonizes over this and is "sick" (according to him). True, we all sin naturally, but we do not commit every kind of sin. I have fellowshipped with thousands of Christians of all ethnic groups for 40 years and feel very comfortable in saying that the vast majority of Christians are not racist. In fact, as I look back over my Christian life, I can honestly say that I cannot think of one racist act imposed upon me by another Christian. This is not to say, however, that there were no racist conversations or events that occurred as I have heard other blacks speak of them. But I personally have not experienced this after being a follower of Jesus Christ for many years, which means, to me at least, that this is not as widespread as many would have us believe; and certainly not the "primary enemy of God's kingdom."

In 2018, Eric Mason, founding pastor of Epiphany Fellowship in Philadelphia Pa published a book entitled, *Woke Church: An Urgent Call for Christians in America to Confront Racism and Injustice.* Pastor Eric states that wokeness means "Holding white people accountable for the racial injustice we are entrenched in." He feels that blacks are being kept in a state of oppression because of the institutions and structures whites have created. Blacks and other minorities need to educate whites, to help them "grow in their racial IQ" so that they can realize that their racism creates the problem. Pastor Eric expresses regret that the Christian Church was not in the forefront of the BLM movement in 1913.

Again, what we see here is a woke ideology which causes division rather than unity. The focus should not be on wokeness, i.e., holding white people accountable for all the racial problems in the world but bringing Christians brothers and sisters together through the gospel and teachings of Jesus Christ, and evangelizing the world.

These are just a few examples of racial/liberal/wokeness ideology in the church but this worldview is far more widespread than we might imagine. In the black churches, this ideology is very common and has a negative impact on the preaching of the gospel of Jesus Christ, and prevents the closeness and unity brethren should have with one another. This ideology in the Black Church is not new but has evolved over time to become what it is today. An extreme example of this is found in what is called Black Liberation Theology.

Black Liberation Theology

Black clergy in many major Christian denominations began to reassess the relationship of the Christian church to the black community shortly after the "black power" movement in 1966. Black caucuses began to develop in the Catholic, Presbyterian, and Episcopal churches, and their mission was to redefine the meaning and role for the church and religion in the lives of black people. Out of this effort came what many call 'Black Theology." Sometimes Black Theology is referred to as Black Liberation theology. For the first time, black theologians, made up primarily of educated, middle-class black clergy, came to believe that there is a need for a completely new starting point in theology. So now they began to re-read the Bible but this time, they would read it through racial lens. This time the Bible would be re-read through the eyes of their slave grandparents which led them to speak of God's solidarity with the oppressed people on the earth; not oppressed by sin necessarily but socially, and economically, and racially oppressed. Right away you can see the problem with this kind of thinking as the primary focus is not on the gospel message, there is a diversion from the gospel. The Bible should be read with our eyes fixed on Jesus (Heb. 12:2) as He alone is the Written and Living Word of God (John 1:1,14; 5:39).

The most prolific proponent and author of the black theological movement was James Cone. Dr. James Cone was a theologian who was best known for his 1969 book entitled *Black Theology* and has been unmatched in his sheer volume of writings and the challenge posed by his writings, and his influence, which is still felt today throughout the nation and other developed countries, among many black Christian theologians and lay members in the church. While many blacks have been influenced by Cone's work, it is worth noting that his work has been criticized inside and outside the African American community. Nevertheless, according to Dr. CF. Eric Lincoln and Lawrence H. Mamiya, in 1990 over one-third of Black clergy have been influenced by Cone's teachings. Speaking of racial prejudice he experienced while growing up in Bearden, Arkansas, Cone said, "It is this common experience among black people in America that Black Theology elevates as the supreme test of truth. To put it simply, Black Theology knows no authority more binding than the experience of oppression itself. This alone must be the ultimate authority in religious matters."

Cone is saying that the black experience of oppression is the real ultimate authority in theology. Of course, this is a distorted view of Scripture. He goes on to say, "It is true that the Bible is not the revelation of God, only Christ is. But it is an indispensable witness to God's revelation." Also, "We should not conclude that the Bible is an infallible witness."

How can Cone seriously dismiss the Bible as the revelation of God and in the same breath state that only Christ is, when as we've shown above, both the Bible and Christ are the Word of God? And there can be no contradiction between the two because God cannot contradict His Word (1 Cor. 14:33). Cone believes that the true meaning of Scripture is not found in the words of Scripture but in the power of the words to point beyond itself to the reality of God's "revelation" and this is to liberate blacks from oppression. He sees Christ as that revelation and Christ was "oppressed" as blacks are today. Christ is "truly God and truly man" but the role of Jesus as God-Incarnate was to liberate the oppressed. Jesus Christ "is God himself coming into the very depths of human existence for the sole purpose of striking off the chains of slavery, thereby freeing man from ungodly principalities and powers that hinder his relationship with God."

This is indeed a sad situation when we have a Christian theologian who blatantly distorts the Word of God by writing and teaching so many untruths about the Bible. He even states that we should not conclude that the Bible is in infallible witness. What? Jesus said, "Your Word is Truth" (John 17:17) and the Bible is the Word of God (2 Tim. 3:16). The Psalmist said the sum of God's Word is truth (Psalm 119:160) meaning the Bible as a whole is true and accurate, no errors. Furthermore, we read in the Scriptures that it is impossible for God to lie (Heb. 6:18). The Bible is the Word of God and God cannot err; therefore, the Bible cannot error. When Cone reads the Scriptures and reaches the type conclusions that he has, it is clear that he is being inspired by someone other than the Holy Spirit.

Isn't Christianity the White Man's Religion?

Malcolm X and those in the Nation of Islam have made it clear that Christianity is the "white man's religion." A considerable number of religious blacks have said that they cannot become a

Christian because Christianity is a "white man's religion." There are Christians who have left traditional Christianity and became Muslims or members of other black religious organizations because they were influenced by this teaching. However, Christians are to always look for the truth and when there are two or more views claiming to be true, then we should prayerfully look at the evidence for each view and go where the most compelling evidence leads. When someone makes a statement that "Christianity is the white's man's religion" that person is making a truth claim. Since that person is making a truth claim, he should provide evidence to support that claim. If that evidence is debunked or otherwise proven false, then we should dismiss that truth claim as false. So, let's look at two of the common reasons why some people believe that Christianity is the white man's religion, and provide a counter perspective as evidence for each of these.

1. Some Christians hold this belief because the name "Adam" as described in *Strong's Concordance* indicates that he was white. Strong describes this kind of man as being ruddy, to show blood in the face, i.e., to blush or turn ruddy. And, they feel, to blush or show blood in the face, is confined to the white race. The problem at the beginning is there is not one iota of evidence to support this view. According to the *Bible Knowledge Commentary,* the Hebrew word for Adam is related to the word for ground as God created Adam from the dust of the ground or we could say clay, which was probably red. But ground or red clay, we know that ground is not white so Adam's name in no way indicates his race or color. To say that Christianity is the white man's religion because Adam and Eve were white is reading into the text something that is not there and is based on pure speculation and conjecture.

2. There are those who say Christianity is the white man's religion because the Jews were white, but again, there is no evidence to support this, biblically, historically, or otherwise. On the contrary, there are a variety of reasons why we know the Jewish people were not white, some are as follows:

- Abraham, the founder of the Jewish nation was from Ur which is modern-day Iraq. Based on the geographical location of Iraq, there is no reason to believe Abraham was any different than the typical Arab today.

- The Israelites spent 400 years in Egypt so there would certainly have been some intermarrying during this long period of time as the order forbidden intermarrying was not given until they had left Egypt.

- The Israelites left Egypt with a diverse group of people, a "mixed multitude went up with them (Exo. 12:38). *Wycliff Bible Commentary* says this mixed multitude refers to "Egyptians and probably other nationalities who had married Hebrews."

- At least two of the twelve tribes of Israel were certainly African. When Joseph was in Egypt, he married "Asenarth who was the daughter of Potiphera, priest of On (Gen. 41:50). Potiphera and his daughter were obviously Egyptian, which means they were Africans; and they hey had two sons, Ephraim (Gen. 41:51-52) and Manasseh (Num 13:4-15).

Furthermore, some members of the twelve tribes intermarried with the Canaanites who were the original inhabitants of the land. The Canaanites were descendants of Canaan, the son of Ham who was the father of the African nations. God had commanded the Israelites not to marry or intermingle with the Canaanites because they served pagan gods (Deut. 7:3). Nevertheless, we know that the Israelites continuously disobeyed God throughout their history, including the order to not marry the Canaanites, and married them anyway (Ezra. 9:1-2). As shown in Chapter 4, Moses married a Cushite woman (Exo. 2:21) and Cushite were black without a doubt. Judah married a Canaanite woman (Gen. 38:2) and then also fathered twins, Perez and Serah, by his daughter-in-law Tamar. Perez's descendants included King David and Jesus (Matt. 1:3-16); and Simeon also had a Canaanite wife (Gen. 46:10).

Clearly, the Israelites were not white, but people of color. And Jesus, the Founder of Christianity was certainly not white as we've demonstrated in Chapter 4 of this book. Therefore, to say that Christianity is the white man's religion is not a true statement. Furthermore, even today, the majority of Christians are people of color, not white. According to Pew Research, there were an estimated 70 million Christians in China alone in 2011. In just ten combined African countries in Sub-Saharan African, the population of Christians is over 377 million. Ten combined countries in the Asia-Pacific have a Christian population of 258 million. This statistic compares to the 246 million Christians in America. In addition to showing that the people of the Bible were people of color, from statistical research, we also see that the assertion that Christianity is a white man's religion is false.

For Pastors, Preachers, and Teachers

As follows of Jesus Christ who have been entrusted with the Word of God, we are admonished to adhere to the Holy Bible in our preaching and teaching of the gospel of Jesus (2 Tim. 4:2; Mark 16:15). Furthermore, we are to add nothing to it or take anything away from it (Deut. 4:2; Rev. 22:18-19). This does not mean that we are to neglect or ignore any topics or issues that come about because the Bible has a perspective on everything, and we are to live by every Word that comes out of the mouth of God. It does mean, however that when we preach and teach, we are to address all topics, subject matter, and issues from a biblical perspective. This means that we are to search the Scriptures to see what God says about various issues that come up and address those issues according to His Word. It means that we are to use love, justice, honest, integrity, and civility in applying the Word of God to these issues and follow the lead of the Holy Spirit as He directs us and as we convey this knowledge from God's Word. It also means that we are to live by the Word in our own lives and frequently reassess ourselves to see where we are falling short and make the necessary adjustments, that we may be lights to others and glorify our Father in heaven (Matt. 5:16).

For My Black Brothers and Sisters in Christ

It is important that we not hold onto or harbor anger, ill-will, or malice about things from the past but forget about those things and keep moving forward (Phil. 3:13-14). We must always have a forgiving Spirit where we feel we've been wrong (Matt. 6:14). Unforgiveness and pride should never be a part of our lives as we continue this Christian journey together. White people are not our enemies and do not want to be labeled as such and many have bent over backward to show this. Yes, there are some few that are racist just as there are some blacks that are racist, but this should not surprise us in the least, as we are told in the Scriptures that there will be enemies among us and outside of us (1 John 2:18; John 15:18-19). However, these are a relatively small percentage, and the overwhelming majority of whites are not our enemies, and we should never hold them accountable or ask them to repent or feel guilty for what their ancestors did in the past. Simply put, it is not their fault, any more than it's our fault for what our ancestors may have done. We are to love our white brothers and sisters in Christ, unite with them, support them, protect, and defend them. And even with those who are non-Christians, we should not look at ourselves as victims and them as victimizers.

For My White Brothers and Sisters in Christ

You should never walk around feeling guilty of what your ancestors did in the past as you had not one shred of control over their activities. You have no need to repent of anything that they did as the Bible does not support such a notion. Of course, you may feel some sense of remorse as a result of their adverse actions towards blacks as we all would feel about any atrocities imposed upon others, whether today or in the past. However, this does not mean that you are to carry guilt around with you for what your ancestors have done; and you should not live your life as a child of God, feeling condemned as God is not condemning you for your ancestors past behavior (Rom. 8:1). The key is for you to live a godly life, walk uprightly, and avoid evil actions on your own accord (Prov. 16:17).

For the Church as a Whole

Jesus' final prayer before His crucifixion was a prayer for unity. Notice what He said:

"I do not pray for these alone, but also for those who will believe in Me through their word; that they all may be one, as You, Father, *are* in Me, and I in You; that they also may be one in Us, that the world may believe that You sent Me. And the glory which You gave Me I have given them, that they may be one just as We are one: I in them, and You in Me; that they may be made perfect in one, and that the world may know that You have sent Me, and have loved them as You have loved Me (John 17:20-23).

This prayer that Jesus delivered to the Father was not only for his disciples at that time but for all who would be followers of Him

– all of us who make up the church today. This means that we are to work together to make this a reality in the church. Jesus sent the Holy Spirit to indwell each of us and help us in accomplishing this unity. He also gave us the Holy Bible to teach us how to go about achieving this. We must keep in forefront of minds that "whites" or "blacks" are not the true enemy that we are being confronted with here. The real enemy behind this entire racial/liberation/woke movement is Satan and his demonic forces in high places (Ephes. 6:12). We must not let race, racism, liberalism, and wokeness prevent us from being the answer to the prayer for unity that Jesus prayed.

For Those Who are Not Christians

In today's culture, you've no doubt seen, heard, or maybe even been a perpetrator of racism or racist acts. You've probably seen efforts to eradicate these acts and hoped that someday, somehow, someone would do something to bring peace to this world and peace to you. Well, we can say unequivocally that there is someone who is in the process of fulfilling that hope. His name is Jesus and there will never be peace on this earth until He returns, as He is the Prince of Peace (Isa. 9:6); and human beings do not know the way to peace (Rom. 3:17). In the meantime, you can have peace within yourself right now and gain a greater understanding of the Creator of the universe and all there is, who loves you with love that is so great, so lofty, so high that it is not fully comprehended by humans. And all you have to do is simply ask God to forgive you of your sins, accept Jesus as your Lord and Savior, and ask Him to come into your life and take control. Then find a local Christ-centered, Bible teaching church that you can attend and allow God to show you His will for your life. You will experience the joy, peace, and contentment that only comes from

God and you will have eternal life with Him in His Kingdom.
Halleluiah!

BIBLIOGRAPHY

Books

Dr. H.C. Felder, *The African American Guide to the Bible*; The Second Edition. Christian Faith Publishing, 2018.

Kerby Anderson, *Christian Ethics in Plain Language*; Thomas Nelson Inc.; 2005.

Candace Owens, *Blackout*; Simon & Schuster Inc. 2020.

David Horowitz, *Dark Agenda*; The War to Destroy Christian America; Humanix Publishing, LLC 2018..

Dr. Jason D. Hill, *We Have Overcome; An Immigrant's Letter to the American People;* Post Hill Press, 2018.

Dr. Norman Geisler, and Dr. Frank Turek; *I don't Have Enough Faith to be an Atheist.* Crossway Books, 2004.

David Barton, *American History in Black and White*; Wallbuilders, Inc. 2004.

Dr. Owen Strachan, *Christianity and Wokeness*; Salem Books, 2021.

Vince Everett Ellison, *The Iron Triangle*; Outskirts Press; 2020.

Mark R. Levin, *American Marxism*; Simon and Schuster, 2021.

Heather McDonald, *The War on Cops*; Encounter Books, 2016.

Dr. Norman Geisler, *A Popular Survey of the Old Testament*, Baker Books, 1977.

Dr. John F. Walvoord and Dr. Roy B. Zuck; *The Bible Knowledge Commentary, New Testament;* David C. Cook, 1983.

Dr. John F. Walvoord and Dr. Roy B. Zuck; *The Bible Knowledge Commentary, Old Testament;* David C. Cook, 1985.

Wilfred Reilly, *Hate Crime Hoax, How the Left is Selling A Fake Race War,* Regnery Publishing, 2019.

Dr. Henry Louis Gates, Jr.; The *Black Church, This Is Our Story, This Is Our Song'* Penguin Press, 2021..

Charles F. Pfeiffer, *The Wycliffe Bible Commentary*: Old Testament (Chicago Moody Press, 1962

Articles and Websites

An Act to Preserve Racial Integrity; http://www2.vcdh.virginia.edu/lewisandclark/students/projects/monacans/Contemporary_Monacans/racial.html

https://www.history.com/search?q=mayflower%20compact

https://www.history.com/news/9-things-you-may-not-know-about-the-declaration-of-independence

Wallbuilders, America's Exceptional History of Anti-Slavery; April 6, 2020

https://www.nasa.gov/topics/universe/features/micro20120111.html

The Census of Marine Life | Smithsonian Ocean (si.edu)

https://www.si.edu/spotlight/buginfo/bugno

American Anthropological Association Statement on "Race", May 17, 1998

John Bickley, 6 Facts From New Study Finding NO RACIAL BIAS Against Blacks In Police Shootings, Dailywire.com; July 11, 2016

https://www.thoughtco.com/white-privilege-definition-3026087.

Wallbuilders, Did America Create Slavery? June 29, 2020

David Emory, 9 Facts About Slavery They Don't Want You To Know; August, 17, 2016.

"Trans-Atlantic Slave Trade – Estimates," Slave Voyages, https://www.slavevoyages.org/assessment/estimates.

Matt Rooney, Everything is Racist: The Definitive List, Save Jersey, July 18, 2019.

Ryan Saavedra, The Congressional Black Caucus Seems To Be Refusing Membership To Black Republican Byron Donalds, June 9, 2021, DailyWire.com

Tami Luhby, These charts show how economic progress has stalled for Black Americans since the Civil Rights era, CNN, July 5, 2020.

Susan Willke Enouen, Research Shows Planned Parenthood Expands Targeting Minorities as it Spurns Racist Founder, September 23, 2020.

Thomas Catenacci, Homicides Have Skyrocketed in These 6 Democratic Cities. Black People Are Disproportionately the Victims, Data Shows, June 24, 2021

Scott Winship, Richard V. Reeves, and Katherine Guyot; The inheritance of black poverty: It's all about the men; Thursday, March 22, 2018.

Department of Justice News Release, Attorney General Holder Statement on the Conclusion of the Grand Jury Proceeding in the Shooting of Michael Brown, November 24, 2014.

Heather Mac Donald, The Ferguson Effect, The Washington Post July 21, 2016.

Jemima McEvoy, At Least 13 Cities Are Defunding Their Police Departments, August 13, 2020.

Democracy Now, Independent Global News, Rep. Ilhan Omar Backs Ballot Initiative to Abolish Minneapolis Police & Create New Public Safety Department, August 5, 2021.

Sarah Elbeshbishi Mabinty Quarshie, Fewer than 1 in 5 Support 'Defund the Police' Movement, USA TODAY/Ipsos Poll finds, March 7, 2021.

Christopher F. Rufo, Critical Race Theory: What It Is and How to Fight It, Imprimis, Volume 50, Number 5, March 2021.

Robert B. Charles, Critical Race Theory, Seven Hard Truths, AMAC Vol. 15 Issue 4.

Christopher F. Rufo, Critical Race Theory: What It Is and How to Fight It, Imprimis, Volume 50, Number 5, March 2021.

Matt Slick, CARM, What is Cancel Culture, January 5, 2021.

Peter Moore, Overwhelming opposition to reparations for slavery and Jim Crow, June 2, 2014.

Kevin D. Williamson, The Case for Reparations, May 24, 2014.

Lucas E. Morel, A Review of the 1619 Project Curriculum, December 15, 2020.

Wilfred Reilly, https://factsandcoffee.com/?p=11, What's Wrong with the 1619 Project? – Facts and Coffee…Your Morning Briefing; January 27, 2021.

Christopher F. Rufo, Ibram X. Kendi is the false prophet of a dangerous and lucrative faith, July 22, 2021.

Intervarsity Urbana Student Missions Conference; https://urbana.org/about-urbana.

Ron Rhodes, Black Theology, Black Power, and the Black Experience, Part two in a Three-Part Series on Liberation Theology.

H.C. Felder, Is Christianity the White Man's Religion? https://ses.edu/is-christianity-the-white-mans-religion/

ABOUT THE AUTHOR

Tom Logan is Associate Pastor of Faith Outreach Community Church in Fort Washington, MD. Pastor Tom has diplomas in Christian Apologetics from the International Institute of Christian Apologetics, The RZIM Academy, and the Reasons Institute. He is also Certified to teach Bible Prophecy by the School of Prophets Institute under Louisiana Baptist University. He has received Certifications for Christian Counseling in a variety of areas from the American Association of Christian Counselors. He graduated from South Carolina State College with a Bachelor's Degree in Business Administration in 1972; and holds Master's Degrees in both Accounting and Taxation from Long Island University. Pastor Tom is a retired Senior Internal Revenue Agent in New York City and Washington DC and lives with his wife Jan in Temple Hills, MD.

Made in the USA
Monee, IL
12 October 2022

15747807R00109